The End of Homework

The End of Homework

How Homework Disrupts Families, Overburdens Children, and Limits Learning

ETTA KRALOVEC AND JOHN BUELL

BEACON PRESS
BOSTON

Beacon Press
25 Beacon Street
Boston, Massachusetts 02108-2892
www.beacon.org

Beacon Press books
are published under the auspices of
the Unitarian Universalist Association of Congregations.

Composition by Wilsted & Taylor Publishing Services

Library of Congress Cataloging-in-Publication Data
Kralovec, Etta.
    The end of homework : how homework disrupts families,
  overburdens children, and limits learning / by Etta Kralovec and
  John Buell.
        p.   cm.
  Includes bibliographical references and index.
    ISBN 0-8070-4218-8 (pbk. : alk. paper)
      1. Homework—Social aspects—United States.   2.
  Education—Parent participation—United States.   3. Home and
  school—United States.   4. Educational change—United States.   I.
  Buell, John.   II. Title.
    LB1048 . K73   2000
    371.3′028′1—dc21

                                                                99-050886

TO CHELSEA AND BRYN MOOSER,
WITH WHOM I SHOULD HAVE SPENT
MORE TIME BAKING COOKIES AND
LESS TIME DOING HOMEWORK.

TO TODD, ELISABETH, AND TIMOTHY
BUELL, IN THE HOPE THAT THEY
WILL BE ABLE TO LIVE IN A WORLD
THAT ALLOWS THEM TO PLACE SEN-
SIBLE LIMITS ON THE WORK OF
THEIR LIVES.

CONTENTS

Beth sits in increasing horror as her daughter's fifth-grade teacher reproaches the class's parents: "Many of the kids have after-school activities like Hebrew school or town soccer league or piano lessons, but you should all remember that homework must always take priority."

Every night Helene dreads coming home to a familiar scene: her fourth-grade daughter sits surrounded by a mess of papers at the kitchen counter, grumpy or weepy, unable to complete her homework and making everyone else share her misery.

Bob hardly ever sees his son, a sophomore in high school who does an average of four hours of homework a night and also works on the school paper, competes in debate, and manages the school track team—all at his guidance counselor's urging. Greg leaves for school at 6:30 A.M., rarely gets home before 6:00 P.M., and almost never joins the family for dinner, since he always has exams to prepare for or papers to write. His weekends are often entirely consumed by meets, debates, and study.

Pat sits in an orthopedic surgeon's waiting room. Her daughter, Anna, has had back pain for quite some time. Pat is convinced that her daugther's thirty-eight-pound backpack is contributing to her daughter's back problems. Anna is not alone. The American Academy of Orthopedic Surgeons (A.A.O.S.) reported that thousands of kids have back, neck, and shoulder pain caused by their heavy backpacks.[1]

Margie phones her best friend Edna practically every night for "help" on the math homework. She really doesn't get fractions. What she really wants are the answers to the problems, and most of the time she gets them. Neither girl wants to cheat, but Margie definitely will get into trouble if she doesn't turn in the homework and Edna just can't say no to her friend.

For the past eight years, we have been writing and speaking about the problems associated with homework. During this time, we have never ceased to be amazed by the strong initial reaction to our work: "What? Are you crazy? Homework is good for kids," or, "How can we compete with the Japanese if our kids don't do homework?" Equally amazing, however, has been the number of folks who eventually come back to us and say, "You're right about one thing: homework is making a mess of our family life."

For a number of reasons, we believe that it is time for a public discussion about the place of homework in the daily lives of schools, children, and families. The topic is central to current debates about school reform. Before we abandon the public school system in favor of some form of privatization, we need to take a hard look at the schooling practices that undermine social life and contribute to a growing sense of alienation and stress in students, their families, and the larger community.

Life for American families has changed dramatically over the past twenty years. The requirements and expectations of the workplace now take up a substantially greater proportion of the adult's day. It's not just the well-documented longer hours but also the cell phone, the portable computer, and e-mail that extend the working day. This phenomenon is an increasingly common topic on talk shows, in news analyses, and at neighborhood barbecues.

Work and schoolwork are part of our system of core values, and they play a vital role in our lives, but they do not define the totality of those lives. It is entirely legitimate and appropriate periodically to question the extent to which even core values should dominate our existence. Discussion about reasonable homework limits is more than just a debate about education; it provides an entrée into other core concerns about our civilization.

We live in dread of what might happen if the enormous homework burden borne by our students and their families was reduced. We fear falling further behind other nations on certain standardized tests. We are afraid our kids won't perform well enough to get into the best colleges. We seem to have lost sight of the importance of family and community life.

If parents were no longer held captive by the demands of their children's schools, they could develop their own priorities for family life. If students were permitted more freedom to structure their own time and to explore their own interests, they would find it much easier to develop both an authentic self and a meaningful social life.

We believe that reform in homework practices is central to a politics of family and personal liberation. Taking back our home lives will allow us to begin the process of enriching our community lives. Drawing a clearer line between the school and the home may enable families to reconstitute themselves *as* families, and help parents pass on to their children something other than the exhaustion of endless work.

"There's just too much," Janet whispered to another mother during soccer practice at their children's elementary school in the coastal community of Blue Hill, Maine. Later that afternoon, over vegetables at the market, Rosalie asked a friend, "Do you think they have too much homework?"

The same question was repeated throughout the community as the amount of homework assigned to the seventh grade kept growing. Finally a group of mothers approached the principal about the issue. Principal Patrick Phillips did what most prudent school administrators would do: he formed a committee.

Fourteen interested members of the school board and the community at large met to grapple with what a small group of parents perceived as the "homework problem." Two key issues lay behind the parents' concern. First was the stress experienced by the middle school students as they tried to balance the demands of homework with extracurricular activities and the need for family time. Second was the inequity inherent in the fact many students lacked the resources at home to compete on an equal footing with those of their peers who had computers, highly educated parents, and virtually unlimited funds for school supplies.

The committee members were charged with formulating a new homework policy that would ultimately be presented to the school board for approval. In late fall 1994, the group identified the major concerns and questions being voiced around town:

What is homework? How much homework is too much? What are and should be the purposes of homework? Can different assignments be given to different kids in one class? Who is responsible for homework—kids or their parents? How is homework graded, scored, or assessed? What about quality versus quantity? How are age and developmental level factored into assignments? Is stress management an issue? How do extracurricular activities—school-sponsored and family-based—factor in? What's the best way to deal with students who put extra time into their work (i.e., the overachievers)? How are assignments coordinated among teachers?

Principal Phillips provided committee members with packets containing the homework policies of schools in surrounding communities, as well as recommendations from organizations such as the National School Boards Association. The real debate began at the next meeting, when members reported that students had said there was more homework in the middle school than at the local high school. The two school board representatives on the committee, the only men other than the principal, stressed the value of homework in instilling a sense of responsibility in students and in helping them learn to budget their time.

The other committee members, mothers all, agreed that responsibility and effective time management were important, but they wondered aloud if there weren't other ways for kids to master those same qualities. Some noted that the vast economic disparity between the richest and the poorest in the community might have a significant impact on the poorer students' ability to do homework. One mother raised the question of the stress caused by excessive homework. On the positive side, a few mothers suggested that when the kids actually completed all their homework, they felt better about themselves.

After two months of meetings, the committee realized that homework was merely a piece of a much larger puzzle: any discussion of homework needed to be coordinated with consideration of many other aspects of the school, including its overall philosophy and value placed on its athletic program, as well as the community's own beliefs about learners.

The school board wanted a new policy to be presented at an early-spring meeting. Anxious to prepare a statement that would reflect the central themes raised in its discussions, the committee went about the task of setting time limits for homework in each grade while stressing the need for equity, coordination, and support for individual differences.

Probably no one was really surprised that the homework time recommendations forwarded to the school board in April 1995 were exactly the same as those put forth in the previous homework policy, adopted in January 1987. Although the new policy was more complete in the sense that it made explicit the concerns raised by the committee, its substance remained unchanged, prescribing so many minutes of homework a night, increasing to one hour by middle school.

According to Blue Hill principal Phillips, homework debates are framed by two often competing American beliefs, the twin demands for excellence and equity in education. Because schools cannot control the home environment, homework raises the profoundly difficult question of how to achieve a level playing field.

Phillips also reflected that the very topic of homework blurred the lines between education and social services. For him, the "homework problem" comprised issues that cast the school in the role of a social service agency, a role he did not feel it should play.

The work of his committee raised the question of the limits of the school's authority and mission, and tested the boundary between the home and the school. While the school's philosophy is based on a belief in the importance of educating the whole child, the committee's work asked, in effect, how we can raise "whole children" when they have little time to do anything other than schoolwork. As Phillips put it, "How can you become a whole person, a sane person? We need to reconsider our time priorities." And yet the new-old policy provided no relief for Janet and Rosalie or their children.

In other communities, the debate has been less restrained than the exchange in Blue Hill. Even as Blue Hill worked through its homework debates, the coastal community of Half Moon Bay, California, was grappling with the same issues. When a school board member there called for an end to homework, Half Moon

Bay got its fifteen minutes of fame: the board member appeared on national television, and the news story was picked up around the world. Headlines on the front page of the *Los Angeles Times* read "Kicking Homework Out of School: Half Moon Bay Considers Abolishing an Educational Icon. Proposal Ignites a Global Storm and Refuels Debate over Whether Such Assignments Really Help."[1]

HOMEWORK AND THE CONTEMPORARY FAMILY

Why write a book about homework? Like mowing the lawn or taking out the garbage, homework seems to be a fact of life. Whether we live in a city, in a small town, on a farm, or in a housing development, when our kids get into school, the homework begins to come home. Parents did their homework in their own day—or didn't do it, but don't tell their children that. We have generally accepted, or at least resigned ourselves to, our kids' having the same obligations.

One reason we have written this book is that the subject of homework is once again on the political agenda in Washington. President Clinton has emphasized the importance of parents' spending more time helping their children with homework. Nonetheless, even as the President and Congress urge us to hit the books with our kids, homework is not always treated with the reverence it was once accorded. In magazines and on TV talk shows and news specials, the common wisdom that more is always better with regard to homework is beginning to be questioned. And if the debates in towns such as Blue Hill and Half Moon Bay are any indication, local school boards are likely to face this issue with increasing frequency in the next few years.

We have found that questioning homework's value nearly always evokes an impassioned response. Challenging the practice requires us to "think outside the box," to use business parlance. And thinking outside the box has never been popular in the world of education. Experimentalism is fine for science and business, the feeling seems to be, but when it comes to the education of our kids, give us the tried and true. Parents survived their own childhood homework experiences and worry if their children aren't exposed to the same demands.

Parents have high aspirations for their children, and homework is one way they believe they can help them get ahead. Teachers have structured their classroom life around homework, and revising the practice would mean changing the very way school operates. Politicians and policy elites have focused public attention on getting students to work harder, rather than on doing something about the deteriorating state of public schooling in America. All of these factors have the effect of closing out the possibility of even discussing the topic.

In order to read this book, you, the reader, must suspend your belief that homework is the sure road to lifetime achievement, and that by helping your child with his or her homework, you are being a responsible parent. This book asks you to examine the effect of homework on the quality of life in your home, especially in your relationships with your children. We are asking that you reflect on the experiences you and your children must forgo to complete homework assignments. We hope that while reading this book, you will open up a dialogue with your children, solicit *their* views on homework, and listen to their concerns. We also recommend that you talk to your friends about the ideas that are presented here.

We all have a sense that things are going terribly wrong in our society. In opening our minds to the possibility that central social practices could be different, we are taking the first step toward change. Maybe the social and economic order we accept as an article of faith makes unreasonable demands of both children and parents. Perhaps children would thrive and even learn better, not only in the long run but even on a day-to-day basis, if they had a little more space for a world of play and fantasy, if their lives were not fully colonized by the demands of schools or parents. It is our conviction that, at the very least, we would all benefit from a sustained consideration of these alternatives. If the case for homework is as solid as its proponents claim, it can stand a little exploratory critique.

HOMEWORK, LEISURE TIME, AND ECONOMICS

Simply put, American parents no longer have the time to give their children the help they need with their homework. The demands made on full-time workers have increased dramatically in the last quarter century, reflecting the ability of corporations to require longer hours; the desperation of employees who are, or who fear, slipping down the economic pyramid; and the decline of organized labor as an effective influence in protecting the rights of workers. Economist Barry Bluestone reports that in the last two decades the average two-earner couple has taken on an additional four months of full-time work outside the home, but has seen only an 18 percent gain in total wages over that same span.[2] The increased transportation, clothing, and child care costs incurred by two-income families mean that most have been barely able to maintain the status quo. And only in the most educated segment of the workforce do two-income families manage to keep pace with inflation.

But if time pressures are *primarily* economic, they also reflect equally broad cultural trends. The two-decade explosion in the rate of divorce and the consequent number of families in which one parent—usually the father—is absent mean that economic, educational, and household responsibilities all fall on the other parent, typically a single mother. Then, too, the kind of community in which that single mother must meet her obligations has itself changed dramatically. The extended family, or even the kind of community in which one knows and trusts one's neighbors, is disappearing. Women who used to be mainstays of their middle-class neighborhoods now work outside the home.

As the old saying goes, the rich have gotten richer. Over the last two decades, the middle class has shrunk. Shifts in the tax burden to the working class, the erosion of tax breaks for families, massive cuts in federal assistance for college, and a new class of the permanently unemployed, characterize contemporary American life. Whereas schools in middle- and upper-middle-class communities may boast computer labs, indoor swimming pools, or state-of-the-art facilities, schools in poor communities may be closed for good due to asbestos contamination. The face they show to the community is boarded-up windows, metal detectors, and chain-link fences. Jonathan Kozol, in his work *Savage Inequalities,* reminds us that differences in income and job security among communities translate into disparities in educational funding and thus into severely unequal educational opportunities.[3]

In the most practical terms, calls for teachers to assign more homework and for parents to provide a quiet, well-lit place for the child to study must always be considered in the context of those parents' education, income, available time, and job security. For many of our fellow citizens, jobs have become less secure and less well paid over the course of the last two decades.

Political or popular reluctance to fund the public schools further exacerbates this situation. As quality and morale deteriorate, parents' dissatisfaction increases, and vouchers and private education become the preferred escape for some. In such a context, policy elites can still insist that schools perform up to standards and that students work as hard as possible both in and out of school. Yet there are reasons to believe that such a strategy will inevitably fail.

Those who demand that our schools employ tougher standards and testing to ensure that American students will measure up to the purported global norm often forget that education is far better supported in other highly industrialized countries. Moreover, these critics are engaged in a kind of apples-to-oranges comparison. In many cases, the foreign students who do best represent a much smaller segment of their nation's population, or are older when they take the tests.

We would argue that homework is likely to become one of the signature issues of the next decade. It is a classic case of an irresistible force meeting an immovable object. The belief of many corporate and business leaders is that the problems of poverty and joblessness can be solved if only our students will study harder and perform better in the workplace. Failing such a miracle cure, these leaders hope to convince a large majority of America that such a course is the only appropriate one in any case, that hard work is the American way, and that it always pays off.

Fortunately or unfortunately, those being asked to shoulder

this burden at home, parents and students, simply cannot rise to the challenge. The time and the cultural and educational resources required are just not there.

We would like to suggest that the inability to meet the challenge of working longer and harder at home may be an opportunity rather than a tragedy. Our own backgrounds in education and political economy have led us to take a longer-term look at the role homework has played in our educational and economic history, at the research on which faith in homework is based, and at the place that homework actually occupies in families embedded within different cultural and economic strata within our society.

Our hope is that by asking readers to contemplate the connections between such seemingly disparate topics as hours at work, the global economy, homework, and the quality of family life, we may initiate a broadly democratic discussion of some of our most fundamental practices and the ways in which they do or do not serve our best interests. If there is one thing we are sure about, it is this: homework has not always played the same role in American life, and the demands we make of our children often reflect the worst as well as the best in ourselves.

CHAPTER I

The Kitchen Table

"Extensive classroom research on 'time on task' and international comparisons of year-round time for study suggest that additional homework might promote U.S. students' achievement."[1] This written statement by some of the top professionals in the field of homework research raises some difficult questions. More homework *might* promote student achievement? Are all our blood, sweat, and tears at the kitchen table over homework based on something that merely *might* be true? Our belief in the value of homework is akin to faith. We assume that it fosters a love of learning, better study habits, improved attitudes toward school, and greater self-discipline; we believe that better teachers assign more homework and that one sign of a good school is a good, enforced homework policy. Recent arguments in favor of homework have stressed its value in strengthening the relationship between home and school and increasing communication between parents and teachers.

Until recently, one could barely pick up a newspaper or magazine for parents without finding yet another educator extolling the virtues of homework. In 1998, however, the spell was broken by a *Newsweek* cover story entitled "Homework Doesn't Help." In outlining research findings that suggested homework is "generally pointless until middle school,"[2] the article provided a breath of fresh air for many parents of elementary school children, though it did not pose the hard questions we must now begin to consider.

How do we know, for example, that homework helps at any level? And helps do what? Raise test scores? Make our children better people, or better citizens? Enable them to become more creative? Develop an interest in lifelong learning? And compared to what? Is it better to do homework or watch TV? Play outside? Go on a trip with parents and siblings? Daydream? Work in the community? Visit with friends? And what does "better" mean in this context, anyway?

THE HOME FRONT

"With few exceptions educators have not thought to look into the home and the interactions between family members for learning about how homework is handled."[3] So wrote three researchers who studied the problem in the mid-1980s. Another thoughtful appraisal came from New York State's Teacher of the Year for 1990:

> [Schools] separate parents and children from vital interaction with each other and from true curiosity about each other's lives. Schools stifle family originality by appropriating the critical time needed for any sound idea of family to develop—then they blame the family for its failure to be a family. It's like a malicious person lifting a photograph from the developing chemicals too early, then pronouncing the photographer incompetent.[4]

Belief in the value of homework is so firmly entrenched that most families accept without question this nightly ritual. For many, it becomes a tug of war between tired parents and children. Every parent knows the frustration and anger that often follow: we cajole, yell, negotiate, compromise, and often bribe in order to see to it that homework is done.

Does this sound familiar? It's six o'clock and the family is gathering at home after the workday. The children are hungry and tired, as are their parents. Dinner must be prepared and cleaned up after, the house must be tended to, and evening chores must be completed. But first there's homework. Help with dinner? "Can't, Mom, I've got too much homework," comes the reply as the child disappears behind a stack of books. Clear off the table so everyone can eat? "Can't, Dad, it's my science project, I can't move it."

Those of us lucky enough to be able to sit down after dinner with the day's paper and our feet up are often called back to work: "I need help memorizing these vocabulary words." "I can't find the answer to this question in my textbook." "I *can't* get off the phone, Dad. I'm trying to get the answer to a math problem."

Regardless of the kind of family we are—with one parent or two, with or without an extended family or siblings, urban or rural, with one or two parents in the paid work force—the story is essentially the same. Bring any group of parents together and the talk will eventually turn to the problems they face in coping with homework. A recent survey conducted by the Public Agenda found that homework is indeed a hot topic with parents: "In focus groups, many parents question whether the work is actually necessary and wonder whether it cuts into 'quality time' that's in short supply in two-income households."[5] It's time for us to ask ourselves why we seem to regard homework as an ugly fact of nature, like the weather or a cold we must endure. Why are we so willing to put up with the imposition of homework on our family lives when we all feel so frustrated about the practice? Are these concerns trivial? Should parents brush aside a bit of impatience and fatigue and get down to work with their kids—even try to use homework as a bonding opportunity—instead of whining to each other about the burden? Perhaps; but first they should ask some tough questions about the assumptions surrounding homework loads.

THE HOMEWORK MYTHS

Many of us continue to supervise homework because we have been led to believe that homework helps boost academic achievement. In fact, findings on the relationship between homework time and academic achievement are conflicting and misleading.

David Davenport, president of Pepperdine University, has raised some serious questions about the efficacy of such thinking. In editorials published in papers around the country, Davenport challenged the practice of accelerating learning through increased homework time and high school advanced placement classes.[6] He argued that summer school enrichment programs that assigned hours of homework robbed students of the time and opportunity to develop in other ways: "Doing homework every night might not be as important as going to a Bible study class or to Girl Scouts. Working in an ice cream store or volunteering at a hospital might be as much of a learning experience as collecting six units of college credit in eleventh grade."[7]

Beyond academic achievement, many teachers and parents see other benefits in homework. Its proponents claim that homework fosters self-discipline, good work habits, and responsibility while at the same time providing accountability, enabling parents to know what is happening during the school day. Researchers, even proponents of homework, point out, however, that "for each potentially positive impact of parental involvement in homework, there [is] a corresponding potential negative effect."[8] Let's look at some of these.

Research shows that personal responsibility is learned from homework only if *parents* systematically structure and supervise homework with that goal in mind.[9] Although we may wish that we could always do that, most parents are just too tired at night, and too busy holding their households together, to structure their evenings around homework.

Most parents would agree that the qualities of character that homework is supposed to encourage are important, but many of us would like to set the agenda for our children's learning them ourselves. Self-discipline, for instance, can be acquired in a variety of ways. Whether it can be imparted through assignments imposed by teachers is an open question, since by definition self-discipline is the ability to take control of one's own actions. As one researcher remarked, "Self-discipline can probably best be learned by taking a cold shower daily, but we don't mandate that."

Lyn Corno, a professor of education at Teachers College, Columbia University, suggests:

> There are a lot more things that parents need to attend to in the upbringing of children in these slippery areas of discipline and personal responsibility that cannot be handled through the reference task of

homework. Homework is but one small piece of a bigger pie in this case. . . . Rather than perpetrating myths about homework, perhaps we should consider some alternative perspectives that research has shown to be closer to reality.[10]

Good work habits are often touted as a favorable byproduct of homework:

> After all, schoolwork is to the child what paid work is to the adult. Because schoolwork also involves homework—the bringing home of work—it means that the youngster is under steady pressure. When children learn to handle the pressure of this job, they are also developing sound work habits.[11]

But do we really believe that learning how to handle work pressure is an appropriate goal for a fourth-grader, or indeed for a child of any age? The implicit assumption here is that we learn best how to handle pressure by *having* to handle it at an early age.

Since the nineteenth century, developmental psychology has been moving away from the notion that children are nothing more or less than miniature adults. In suggesting that children need to learn to deal with adult levels of pressure, we risk doing them untold damage. By this logic, the schoolyard shootings of recent years may be likened to "disgruntled employee" rampages.

Many of us would question whether our fighting with our children for twelve years about homework could possibly foster good habits. In contrast, participating in the decisions of the household and collaborating with others on common chores, from cooking to cleaning to doing routine repairs, are important life skills that also require good work habits. For many children, these habits are never learned because homework gets in the way of that work.

Other children fail to complete their homework precisely because they have obligations that are far more pressing, such as looking after younger siblings or aging grandparents. Some have children of their own to care for after school; others must prepare dinner for their families. These students are faced with an agonizing choice between meeting their familial responsibilities and meeting their school responsibilities. Even those children who are able to complete both household chores and homework face painful choices regarding social, recreational, and other nonacademic opportunities, choices that doubtless leave a bitter taste.

Most proponents of homework suggest that better time management by parents can solve most homework problems. Many of us have been told by our children's teachers that all we need to do is set up a rigorous homework schedule and see that it is kept—no easy task in itself. The market for self-help books and tutors continues to grow as homework demands increase.

In this regard, discussions about homework mirror a range of contemporary issues. Everything from teenage pregnancy to success in the workplace is treated as a matter that can be reduced to an equation of individual responsibility. Yet as the number of books written about how to combine homework with a satisfying family life proliferates, isn't it reasonable to ask whether there is an issue here that goes beyond how well we as individuals monitor our time or discipline our children? To borrow the language of the great radical sociologist C. Wright Mills, when millions experience difficulties within the privacy of their own homes, perhaps we need to ask why homework too often appears to be a private trouble rather than a public issue.[12] How disheartening it is, then, that there are over a hundred books available on how to help a child with his or her homework, but not one that asks whether we as families ought collectively to revise or reform these shared demands.

Many people feel that substantial homework is the sign of a good teacher and that it provides a system of accountability for parents. In this view, homework is seen as a way to assure parents that there are "standards" in place, though in fact it often has the opposite effect. Many of us see the work that comes home with our children and wonder if this is really the best the system has to offer.

Some of the most expert teachers regard rigid homework policies as undermining their professional judgment, their curricular goals, and their teaching efficacy.[13] These teachers often seek more innovative and individualized approaches to homework, and their motives are commendable. Nonetheless, even innovative homework can have its pitfalls. Much in vogue these days is the practice of giving more imaginative, complicated homework assignments, such as family-history projects or "family math" problems. These challenging assignments may be viewed by parents as an indication that the school is doing some interesting things. A closer inspection, however, may reveal some shaky underpinnings.

When your child brings that science-fair project home, for example, what happens? Completing this kind of project requires sophisticated research skills, including knowing how to frame research questions; how to establish a time frame for the work; how to analyze evidence at various stages; how to synthesize findings; and how to present the material in an attractive fashion. Often students are given no professional guidance in these matters but are instead sent home with a dictate: Do a science-fair project in four weeks. As parents, we are led to ask, Whose job is it to teach our children? Some of us see such homework assignments not as a sign that the school is doing a good job, but rather as an indication that it has ceded its responsibility for teaching to the parents. Rather than *providing* accountability, this kind of homework allows schools to *shift* accountability to the parents.[14] The parents are expected to oversee the science experiment, furnish the necessary materials, help interpret findings, and supply guidance on how to complete the project. We have become accountable for our children's learning. To whom, then, is the school itself accountable?

The increased emphasis on parental "involvement" in homework is reflected by a program that is now being widely implemented: Teachers Involve Parents in Schoolwork (TIPS). Like a number of other educational innovations, it is the subject of national workshops, workbooks, and videos. The concept is straightforward: the program requires students to explain and demonstrate something interesting they are learning in class to someone at home.[15] Simple idea, right? Who could complain? But again, there's more to it than meets the eye.

In a research report on TIPS, a team of its proponents found that students enjoyed the program and that parents felt more involved in and more knowledgeable about what their children were learning. The researchers' conclusion, however, could hardly serve as a rallying cry:

> In this study, interactive homework that involved family members influenced or increased students' homework completion and helped students improve their skills and report card grades *somewhat*, but classroom teaching must improve dramatically to increase students' writing skills and progress to meet high standards. Motivating and challenging lessons and activities are needed every day of every year in school for students to gain and maintain language arts skills.[16] [emphasis added]

And this statement was written by people who pushed for the program!

The plea for improvements in classroom teaching practice is lost in the avalanche of material disseminated by the U.S. Department of Education on behalf of initiatives such as TIPS.[17] In this context, we may also ask how much a TIPS program costs a school, and what other budget items must be eliminated to make room for it. Whose interests are served when a school buys into such a program? Why does the U.S. government support this initiative? Some more cynical researchers suggest that any program that focuses attention on student learning will show increases in that learning, not necessarily because the program itself is effective but rather because personal attention is being paid to the learner.

Another program, called Homelinks, is an interactive homework initiative used around the country. This program asks parents to guide elementary school students through thirty minutes' worth of homework in a different subject area each night of the week. Homelinks offers workshops to help parents learn how to help their children—provided, of course, that the parents can find the time to take the workshops.

Yet another program calls for students to carry a planner home to be signed by a parent on a nightly basis. This and other, similar programs are part of a national movement toward more creative homework, sparked in part by a 1996 research report by Gary Natriello and Ed McDill.[18]

Ironically, as a parent, Natriello shortly thereafter found himself having to live with his own policy recommendations. After establishing a time and place for homework and working through the directions with his child as he and McDill had advised, he noted that

> not only was homework being assigned as suggested by all the "experts," but the teacher was obviously taking the homework seriously, making it challenging instead of routine and checking it each day and giving feedback. We were enveloped by the nightmare of near total implementation of the reform recommendations pertaining to homework. . . . More creative homework tasks are a mixed blessing on the receiving end. On the one hand, they, of course, lead to higher engagement and interest for children and their parents. On the other hand, they require one to be well rested, a special condition of mind not often available to working parents. . . . I am probably on the high end of the scale of parental commitment. . . . I am also way up there in terms of support for higher-order learning. But I have recently learned firsthand the limitations of my ardor. To put it plainly, I have discovered that after a day at work, the commute home, dinner preparations, and the prospect of baths, goodnight stories, and my own work ahead, there comes a time beyond which I cannot sustain my enthusiasm for the math brain teaser or the creative story writing task.[19]

Natriello still seems rather good-humored about the whole thing, but then, when he wrote this, his kids had yet to reach middle school.

Like Natriello, who viewed homework differently from the "receiving end," other researchers are moving beyond dogma and rhetoric about homework by suggesting that when we look at the environment in which homework is actually done, we begin to get a very different picture of the practice:

> In going directly to homework scenes for guidance on how to understand homework, the relevance of the categories [i.e., motivation,

achievement, and skill] with which homework is normally understood seemed to disappear. . . . These categories did not tell us much
about what was going on in homework.²⁰

It isn't simply the fatigue factor that keeps these programs from
having the desired outcomes. Another important factor can be a
lack of parental training or facility with the assignment, or in-
adequate resources at home to complete a project satisfactorily.
The home environment is fundamentally different from the classroom.

Some educational researchers are interested in the learning
that goes on in families, and especially in how children are taught
to be members of a family and to live within a particular community. This kind of teaching and learning is contrasted with the
kind necessary to mobilize the family for homework, wherein the
home environment is given over to "playing school." During this
time, any difficulties the child experiences in school are re-created
in the home as the parent plays the role of teacher and the child
again becomes the student. When homework is examined in this
light, the researchers conclude, the following questions arise:

> What pressures are constraining families to organize such regressive
> homework scenes, and what would have to be reorganized to change
> them for the better? What can parents do to keep homework from
> disrupting family relations? What can parents do to protect a child
> they have not been able to help at home?²¹

This list suggests a very different landscape from that sketched
by the kinds of questions that are usually associated with homework. This research alerts us to the possible negative impact of
homework. In this context, the center of gravity in the homework debate shifts from the assumption that parents must conform
to schools' homework standards to the notion that homework
affects families in myriad ways. Maybe it is time for parents finally
to admit that even with the best intentions, the most perfectly organized homework schedule, a "quiet place to study," and rigid
homework rules, homework disrupts family life beyond a tolera-
ble limit.

THE TIME SQUEEZE

It is generally agreed that time has become a hot commodity. With everyone working longer and longer hours, and with more women than ever in the workplace, time itself has become more precious than ever. Since the early nineties, this trend has been a topic of extensive media coverage. Beepers, cell phones, and e-mail can all be taken as signs that our work lives are encroaching upon our private lives at an alarming rate. In her ground-breaking work on the subject, *The Overworked American,* Juliet Schor argues that the unexpected decline of leisure has had profound effects on our lives. Americans are now working longer hours than workers in any other industrialized nation. By 1989, for example, U.S. manufacturing employees were working 320 hours—the equivalent of about two months—a year more than their counterparts in West Germany or France.[22] The phenomenon is so striking that researchers now talk about "time poverty."[23] The increase in working hours, longer commutes, and the fact that many more mothers now work outside the home all affect the household in ways we are just beginning to comprehend. Some experts believe that women bear the brunt of the time squeeze because they take on a disproportionate share of the household work.[24] And time is tightest of all for heads of single-parent households.

In 1970, some 42 percent of mothers with children under the age of eighteen were in the labor force; by 1980 that figure had risen to 56.6 percent. By 1998, the last year for which complete statistics are available, the percentage of women with children under the age of eighteen in the paid labor force had risen to 71.8 percent. Increasing numbers of these women are also now the sole supporters of their children. The Children's Defense Fund reports that half of all children under eighteen will live in a single-parent household during some point in their childhood.[25] In addition, by most accounts, working women in all circumstances have a "second shift" that accounts on average for another twenty-five to forty-five hours in the home each week.[26]

Schor has properly pointed to the role that the "work and spend" cycle plays in this dynamic. As workers, we seldom have any control over the number of hours we labor in the workplace; at best we can expect increased wages as the productivity of our workplace improves. We could save these wages and hope eventually to escape the workplace, but such an effort would require many years. In any case, there are also immense social pressures to spend money. As Schor's most recent work points out, these include the peer pressures of the workplace itself. Can one hope to climb the corporate ladder—or even retain one's job—if one fails to embrace the life style of the most successful? Consumption becomes, in short, a way to achieve both personal identity and a sense of social connectedness. Unfortunately, it is very unstable ground, as the ante is always being upped and the social and environmental stakes are high.

Paradoxically, the very emphasis on work, wages, and consumption, essentially compulsory within our political economy, also undermines other forms of community and self-expression. We have little opportunity to enjoy recreation, community events, local politics, or family life. Our diminished possibilities in this regard in turn reinforce our reliance on wages and the workplace. And even the family time that remains after the demands of work and commuting are met is increasingly structured by the requirements of the workplace and school.

None of us needs national statistics or sophisticated political analysis to tell us that we have precious few hours of free time with our children, and that what free time we do have is often given over to policing the unfinished work of the school day. The media widely suggest that high school students do no homework. This hardly squares with the experience of many parents. The most thorough survey research, conducted by the University of Michigan's Survey Research Center and recently reported by *Time* magazine, casts serious doubt on the media claim. SRC's detailed time diaries for a large sample of U.S. families focuses on grade school children. For these children, homework has increased to 134 minutes a day from its 1981 figure of 85 minutes. Though Michigan has not yet conducted comparable surveys for high school students, it seems hard to believe increases of a similar magnitude have not occurred at that level. The homework policies with which we are familiar mandate gradually escalating levels of homework as students become older. It seems strange that many mainstream media, which dutifully report as final truth SRC's monthly survey of "consumer confidence," have paid scant attention to their equally thorough surveys of students' working days. It is apparently very easy for many institutions in our society to jump on the bandwagon of blaming kids and demanding ever more homework.[27]

ANY HOME, ANY NIGHT, USA

As dinner ends, the nightly ritual begins. Jesse opens by saying that he left his homework in his locker; he has to be driven to school to pick it up before the dishes get done. When the schoolbooks are on the table, Jesse realizes that his history textbook tells him little of what he needs to know about the economic causes of the Civil War. He calls on his dad for some help. After a long day at work, his dad can barely remember that there *was* a Civil War, much less what economics had to do with it. Together Jesse's father and mother try to piece together the Civil War over dishes and the crying baby. Frustrated, they get angry at Jesse and remind him that he should listen more carefully in class. Jesse assumes his "student" posture and complains that his teacher never teaches anything the class needs to know. "My history teacher is the football coach, he doesn't know anything about the Civil War," adds Jesse, trying to save face.

Jesse's younger brother Matt is struggling with his math. He has twenty-five long-division problems, and he needs help. His mom knows a shortcut for solving them. A fight breaks out between her and Matt because she is doing them in a different way than the teacher illustrated in class. In tears, Matt throws his math book across the dining room and retreats to the TV. And so the evening goes. Both parents occasionally call down to Matt to turn off the TV, but they are more concerned this evening with helping Jesse get his homework right. Finally, giving up in exhaustion, the family goes to bed, often with the homework left undone and the household chores postponed yet again.

Jesse used to be a Boy Scout. With his troop he learned to

camp, read to the elderly, clean up the local river, and chase snakes. When he got to high school, he had to give all that up—no time. We all know that high school kids spend an enormous amount of time at school. Some adults complain that school gets out at 2:15, so the actual school day is not really that long, but when you take into account travel time to and from school and the average two to three hours of homework a night, even kids who don't take part in extracurricular activities have a very long day indeed. And school time always comes at the expense of time spent in other ways.

Embedded in this one story are all the major problems inherent in homework. It interferes with important family and community participation. The parents may confuse the child or be unqualified to help him or her, which causes stress between them. Then, too, the parents are unable to pursue their own educational agenda for their children.

Often, the school time spent within the home not only produces tensions but also fosters educational conflict between school and home. Some conflict is inevitable and even healthy: children, especially as they get older, can benefit from different perspectives and approaches to learning. Nonetheless, when parents are forced to reinforce or reiterate a message they don't understand or cannot accept, the conflict may cease to be a healthy, intellectual one. Many educators have commented on this phenomenon: teachers often complain that parents don't really help their kids, but rather hinder them by getting involved in their homework.[28] Some math and science teachers have even given up assigning homework because when kids do it wrong, the teachers must help them "unlearn" what they learned at home.

Most of us have had the experience of trying to help our children, only to find that our understanding of the material was very different from the information provided in their textbooks. In scanning our children's history texts, for example, we may be startled to discover a slant on history that is quite unlike our own. One professional biologist wondered about the value of the biology text used in his son's eighth-grade class; he was trying to help with homework and when he looked at the biology book, he saw that the science was watered down. "What should I do?" he asked. "If I complain to the school, they'll think I'm a meddling parent. But I can't teach my kids this stuff because it's out of date and in many cases just plain wrong."

The gap between parents' knowledge and understanding and what is taught in school has led some researchers to conclude that homework doesn't always strengthen relations between home and school.[29] Our time with our children is mediated by school knowledge that is often at odds with our own knowledge and beliefs. Many parents come to feel that engaging in a good dinner-table conversation is better for their children than retreating to their rooms to complete worksheets.

We all have educational agendas for our own children. We want them to learn certain things that we believe are important. For some, knowing how to fix a car is a priority; for others, learning to complete household chores conscientiously is essential. One of us wanted her own kids to know how to sew, while a friend felt her children should learn Hebrew. Most of us find we do not have enough time with our children to teach them these things; our "teaching" time is instead taken up with school-mandated subjects. We often wonder if we wouldn't have less tension in our society over prayer in schools if our children had more time for religious instruction at home and for participation in church activities. When school is the virtually exclusive center of the child's educational and even moral universe, it is not surprising that so many parents should find school agendas (with which they may or may not agree) a threat to their very authority and identity.

We all want our children to learn how to take part in the work of the family. Learning to do one's fair share of the housework is something that most of us value. We have all had the experience of asking the kids to do some chore and being told they couldn't because they had too much homework. At that moment, we have to wonder if doing math problems is more important than participating in the life of the family. Constructing and caring for a family take time and effort and must be learned in the doing.

BEYOND HOMEWORK

> Regulations: Meriden Public Schools
> What Teachers Can Expect from Parents Regarding Homework
>   1. Teachers can expect that parents will arrange a quiet suitable place, with adequate workspace, for the youngster to work.
>   2. Teachers can expect that the parents will cooperate by encouraging their youngster to complete homework assignments.
>   3. Teachers can also expect parents to understand the value of various types of homework, since the value differs under different circumstances and conditions.[30]

We are all familiar with statements such as this, sent home by our child's school at the beginning of the year. Most of us just sign the stack of papers and send it back, but maybe we should be looking a little more closely. Notice, for example, that this "regulation" says nothing about what the *parents* can expect from the *teacher*. As parents, we need to set out our position about homework clearly. We should begin to frame a set of hard questions about homework and not accept easy answers. In sum, maybe it's time for regulations about homework written from the parents' point of view. We'll suggest some guidelines in chapter 7.

Last, but perhaps most important, we need to ask about the relationship between the family and the state. We should question whether homework may not represent an intrusion by the state into our private lives. We would hardly stand for a government mandate that we spend an hour each night on citizenship training; the very thought evokes Big Brother. But in essence, that is exactly what the homework ritual is. The school, as an instrument of the state, has invaded our family time with its agenda. Americans cherish their privacy and their individuality. The state can and must establish minimal conditions under which we can thrive as individuals, but it should also allow us as great a range of privacy and individuality as possible. Homework flies in the face of both criteria, becoming a kind of microregulator of the time and content of our interaction with our children. It puts every American family in the position of being servants of the state. Parents are expected to do the unfinished work of the teacher; we are told what we must teach our children and the amount of time we must spend on that teaching. This work is unpaid, and often we are unprepared for it.

The kitchen table has become the landing site of state-mandated curriculum and locally mandated homework policies. The police need a search warrant to enter your house, and in some states you can shoot someone who comes uninvited into your home, but homework finds its way in on the backs of our children and mediates our most intimate time with them. It dictates what we must talk about with our children. Rather than connecting us in a meaningful way with the school, it often alienates us from our children as they are forced to take on their role as student while we don the teacher's cap.

While homework affects all American families, its impact is different for families in different classes. As Americans, we don't like to talk about class, but when we talk about the homework spread over the kitchen table, we have to recognize that some tables are bigger than others. Our class position in this society influences our ability to help our children with their homework in subtle and complex ways. In addition, class determines just what our children's opportunities will be with homework.

The conflicts over homework can often replicate and intensify a set of problems that Richard Sennett referred to as the hidden injuries of class. Many of the parents who struggle over problems with their kids themselves hold down marginal, insecure, and unstimulating jobs within the corporate world. How do they explain or justify to their children the frustrations and limits they face on a daily basis? In a political economy in which broader corporate reform is seldom on the agenda anymore, it becomes too easy to focus on self-blame: *If only I had studied harder or been a better student. . . .* And unfortunately, feeling unable to help one's children, especially relatively young children, can only reinforce this message of self-blame. Much as many business and educational leaders might hope that such parents would draw on their own experience to drive home the message that homework is important, self-hatred all too easily leads to hostility toward others, even toward one's own family.

CHAPTER 2

Does Homework Work?

In the last century, hundreds of studies have been conducted in the United States on homework. Many researchers have examined these studies looking for data to support their belief in the educational value of homework, while a smaller number have searched the same material for data that will prove the thesis that homework is counterproductive to a child's development. Often the same studies are cited to bolster contradictory positions. These findings merit a closer look.

In the first and only major overview of the topic, Harris Cooper analyzed research on homework from the previous fifty years. *Homework* makes worthwhile reading for anyone who is serious about understanding the complexity of research findings on this topic. Cooper explores homework's effects in three different scenarios: homework versus no homework, homework versus in-class study, and time spent on homework compared with achievement. He considers these variables across grade levels, student ability levels, and subject areas.

Cooper lists the following as the major positive and negative effects of homework as identified by educators:

> *Positive Effects of Homework:*
> Immediate Achievement and Learning
> - Better retention of factual knowledge
> - Increased understanding
> - Better critical thinking, concept formation, and information processing

- Curriculum enrichment

Long-term Academic
- Encourage learning during leisure time
- Improved attitude toward school
- Better study habits and skills

Nonacademic
- Greater self-direction
- Greater self-discipline
- Better time organization
- More inquisitiveness
- More independent problem solving

Negative Effects on Achievement and Learning:
Satiation
- Loss of interest in academic material
- Physical and emotional fatigue

Denial of access to leisure time and community activities
Parental interference
- Pressure to complete and perform well
- Confusion of instructional techniques

Cheating
- Copying from other students
- Help beyond tutoring
- Increased differences between high and low achievers[1]

Cooper reports that research on homework, focused primarily on its role in boosting academic achievement, provides little conclusive data to either support or refute its value as a means of improving the academic performance of American schoolchildren: "The conclusions of past reviewers of homework research show extraordinary variability. Even in regard to specific areas of application, such as within different subject areas, grades, or student ability levels, the reviews often directly contradict one another."[2]

The tangle of contradictory research findings and interpretations is a confusing one to sort through. As parents who struggle with this schooling practice, we find little solace in hearing that the findings on homework are inconsistent. We are more than mystified by what this might mean.

Bill Barber, an educational researcher critical of the practice of homework, has undertaken an in-depth study of research findings used to establish the claim that "homework appears to benefit learning, especially if it is graded or commented on."[3] Barber points out that of the fifteen studies on which that claim is based, only one actually measured the relationship described.

"If research tells us anything," he argues, "it is simply that even when achievement gains *have* been found, they have been minimal, especially in comparison to the amount of work expended by teachers and students."[4]

As parents, we would like to think that we may find the "truth" somewhere in the middle of these conflicting claims. However, most educators doubt that is possible. School personnel have an even harder time of it: they must make school policy based on this confusing research picture. In the Connecticut Department of Education's *Manual on Policy Development* (1984), the section on homework begins with the following caveat:

> Educators and lay people alike share the belief that increased emphasis on homework will contribute to better student achievement. In fact, however, there have been few studies on the relationship between homework and student achievement and the studies which have been undertaken have yielded conflicting conclusions. But even if definitive support for homework cannot be found in research, the strong sense that homework is a valuable component in the educational experience of most students means that efforts to increase homework will be mounted.[5]

Because many educational leaders seem unwilling to challenge the taken-for-granted practice of homework, and because educational researchers have politely agreed to disagree, parents are thus faced with enforcing a practice whose value has yet to be proved. As Harris Cooper explains it,

> [First,] many of the studies used poor research designs. The homework question would benefit greatly from some well-conducted, large-scale studies. Second, given the richness of thinking and debate on homework . . . research has been narrowly focused on

achievement as an outcome. Only a few studies looked at home-work's effect on attitudes toward school and subject matter (with generally negligible results.) No studies looked at non-academic outcomes like study habits, cheating or participation in community activities.[6]

HOW GOOD IS THE RESEARCH?

Educational research on the topic of homework is plagued by a number of conditions that further complicate matters. As Cooper points out, the research that has been done has been very limited in scope, looking only at achievement. In this respect, studies of homework illustrate a central failing of much academic research.

The narrow specialization of the academic world has meant that researchers tend to consider only one piece of a problem at a time, in this case homework and its effect on academic achieve-ment. But the issues involved are broader than just school achieve-ment, as Cooper suggests. Recently, researchers in a very different field, that of family studies, have begun to call for a closer look at the "ecology of homework."[7] They insist that homework must be examined in the context of how it affects the organization of the family and the family structure, as well as how its impact is felt across socioeconomic lines.

Another part of the problem that plagues homework research has to do with the very nature of social science itself. Any effort to establish causality in the social sciences will run into several major obstacles. Let's take the example of studies on the relationship be-tween time and learning. Most of us believe that there is a strong link between the time children spend on learning and their level of achievement—that is, the more time our kids are in school and doing homework, the more they will learn. However, most edu-cational researchers urge caution in trying to prove a causal con-nection here.

In one study of learning and time, H. J. Walberg and W. C. Fredrick found that time appeared to be only a modest predictor of achievement. They concluded that though we may all assume that the longer we are in school, the more we will know, we cannot make a causal claim for that thesis: "As the investigators acknowledge, it is difficult to say whether people know more because they attended school longer or attended school longer because they were more capable."[8]

Equally, those who attended school for longer periods may have done so because their work both in school and outside was more stimulating or better supported. In his work on homework, Cooper explored the time-learning link by reviewing the reports of more than half a million students over thirty years and examining twenty-six studies that focused on the relationship between homework time and student achievement. Some studies showed a positive correlation between time and achievement, while others showed a negative correlation. Cooper found that homework's effect on achievement was closely related to grade level, but he cautions:

> If homework is taken as the causal agent, the results suggest that increases in time spent on home study have [a] more positive effect on the achievement of students at higher grades. Increasing the amount of homework for middle-grade students may be efficacious only up to a certain point. There is no evidence that any amount of homework noticeably improves the academic performance of elementary students.[9]

We are advised, even here, against making any causal claim:

> In sum, fifty correlations based on over 112,000 students revealed a positive relation between student reports of time spent on homework and several academic outcomes. However, it is still plausible, based on these data alone, that teachers assign more homework to students achieving better or that better students spend more time on home study.[10]

Cooper's work highlights the difficulty of establishing any causal connections. Time and achievement may indeed be related, but as Cooper points out, we cannot make the claim that homework *causes* the achievement. In the studies that found a positive correlation—that is, that time spent did increase achievement—

teachers may have given more homework to higher-achieving students. In studies that found a negative correlation—that time spent did *not* increase achievement—the brighter students may simply have finished their homework faster. According to Cooper, "Both positive and negative correlations have been found in past research (though positive correlations dominate) and, not surprisingly, each interpretation has been invoked to make sense of the data."[11]

Cooper's work provides us with one more example of a problem that routinely bedevils all the sciences: the relationship between correlation and causality. If A and B happen simultaneously, we do not know whether A causes B or B causes A, or whether both phenomena occur casually together or are individually determined by another set of variables. The only way to move beyond this problem is to specify the variables more clearly. For our purposes, this means conducting in-depth interviews with students and considering the learning process itself in order to understand the role homework, in its many forms, plays in different kinds of academic development. Thus far, most studies in this area have amounted to little more than crude correlations that cannot justify the sweeping conclusions some have derived from them.

Even more fundamentally, the social sciences display a distinctive relation of theory to practice. When social scientists argue that homework improves educational outcomes, for instance, that very theory enters into and affects the environment under study —in contrast to the more concrete world of the natural sciences, where, for example, predictions by astronomers cannot be said to influence the path of the stars. Frequent repetition of the notion that homework is the only way to boost student performance, however defined, cannot help but affect teachers and students. It may deter research into alternative modes of learning or even blind us to the gains that emerge from them. And it may lessen the self-esteem of those who simply can't bear doing endless homework along conventional lines.[12]

None of these caveats is meant to argue against a broad-based social science, one that would supplement correlational studies with more detailed research into students' lives and the learning process. Since correlational studies regarding homework will always suffer from inherent biases related to self-reporting —including the problem of isolating the effects of the parents' education and income from the effects of the student's own motivations—a strong case can be made for the need for both survey research on the effects of homework and ethnographic studies such as the following.[13]

THE CASE OF DANIEL

Most of us do not live our lives according to research findings; rather, we struggle with questions about homework at our kitchen table. For the sake of argument, though, let's take the research findings in their most positive light and assume that yes, homework does boost school achievement for high school students. Then let's turn to an actual case, a story that will probably sound familiar to anyone with children.

Daniel is a sixteen-year-old junior in high school. A typical boy with boundless energy and an unfailing enthusiasm for life, he is an astute observer of human nature, a budding photographer, and an amateur naturalist. He could easily occupy all his free time with reading, exploring tidal flats, and playing with his friends. A member of the soccer and tennis teams, he uses sports to burn off his unused energy after a day of sitting at school desks.

Daniel does satisfactory work in school, primarily as a consequence of a strong dose of parental and peer pressure. Nonetheless, he hates math, and always has. Daniel leaves for school every morning at 6:45 and returns home after sports practice, at around 6:00 in the evening. He usually has between two and three hours of homework each night, much of it algebra II. By the end of the evening, Daniel tends to feel rather low. His inability to complete his math homework causes him to feel stupid. His frustration at not being able to pursue his own interests leaves him hating the "learning" part of school even as he thrives on the sports and social scenes there.

Daniel wants to go to college, but his grades are only so-so. His parents now push a little harder for him to pull up his B− grade average. But Daniel wants to use his evenings to take a photography class at the local university, because he can't fit a photography class into his college prep program at school. He also wants to join a search-and-rescue team. He loves adventure and helping people and thinks it would be "cool" to assist in rescuing stranded climbers in the nearby national park. Daniel doesn't have time to engage in these activities, however, because his weekends are consumed by homework and sports. Daniel's grandfather lives nearby and is getting older; he and Daniel were very close when Daniel was younger, but now they rarely see each other. Daniel just doesn't have time.

Sound familiar? In this scenario, what does increased academic achievement mean? Can we promise Daniel's parents that if he does his homework he will boost his SAT scores or his grades enough to enable him to get into a top college? And if he does get in, will he thrive economically and emotionally for the rest of his adult life? If other families and children make similar sacrifices, will all of them thrive?

Despite the contradictory findings about the relationship between homework and achievement, the lack of research into the nonacademic benefits that homework is purported to provide, and our inability to make solid causal claims about homework's efficacy, it appears that our cultural bias in favor of homework remains firmly in place.

BUT HOMEWORK IS GOOD FOR KIDS

We all want to believe that school systems operate on solid, research-based policies. Nevertheless, the limits of the research conducted to date suggest that when it comes to homework, the real basis of school policy is something else entirely. What are we to make, for example, of the Connecticut Department of Education's promotion of a policy that it acknowledges has no real basis in research? Where do the policymakers get their "strong sense that homework is a valuable component in the educational experience"?

We believe that this "strong sense" can be understood only in the context of the larger culture of schools and the political economy in which they are situated. The widespread concern over recent declines in student achievement reflects more than simply the scores per se; it also mirrors business and government anxieties over the "competitive global economy" and the need to keep American business ahead of other nations'.

Certainly other forces are also at work here, and one of the most powerful is the notion of "tradition." There is a truism in the field of education: Teachers tend to teach the way they were taught. This may help illuminate some of the difficulty we face in getting schools to change. It also explains the sense of comfort we sometimes experience when we walk into a school and find that it smells, looks, and is organized much like the school that we ourselves attended. In those moments we often feel, *Isn't it great that some things never change!* Schooling looks pretty much the same today as it did at the turn of the twentieth century. Sure, the desks used to be bolted to the floors and now they are freestanding, and there may be a few computer in the back, but beyond that it's business as usual. Rather than lulling ourselves into complacency, we should be asking why it is that schools seem to carry on unchanged in spite of all sorts of criticism—from angry parents to research findings condemning educational practices—and efforts at improvement in the form of federal programs.

Remembering that schools are embedded inside the social, political, and economic systems of our country can help us understand the pressures they face to perform certain functions. How does homework fit inside this nested system of often competing agendas? What do teachers see themselves as doing when they assign homework, and what is behind the national trends toward increased homework time?

First we should acknowledge that there are some teachers who question the very practice of homework. Many of them are troubled by the problems inner-city kids have in completing their assignments; others are worried about the erosion of the family due to homework; and still others are concerned about the inequity inherent in the system.[14] Nonetheless, the majority of teachers continue the practice.

In national surveys, teachers have reported the following reasons for their assigning homework:

1. Homework teaches self-discipline. Eighty-eight percent of teachers and principals in one study agreed that homework "develops children's initiative and responsibility."[15]
2. Homework is believed to increase student achievement.
3. Homework fulfills the expectation of students, parents, and the public. Teachers favor the practice by 95 percent, according to a recent Gallup Poll.[16]
4. Homework increases the length of the school day without increasing the number of hours actually spent in school.
5. Homework provides an avenue of communication between the school and the parents.

The belief that homework teaches self-discipline and improves student achievement is firmly entrenched, but as we have seen, these claims are dubious at best.

As more academic demands are placed on teachers, homework can help lengthen the school day and thus ensure "coverage"—that is, the completion of the full curriculum that each teacher is supposed to cover during a school year. For example, we now expect that our children will learn how to use computers in school. But where can time be found for that without dropping something that students were learning before? Making classes a bit shorter to fit in this new requirement often means that the lost instruction time must be made up for by homework.

The pressure on schools to raise standards and to encourage parent participation has also added to the recent push for more homework. Homework is often seen as the parents' eyes and ears on the school. This in itself places pressure on teachers to create meaningful homework and often to assign large amounts of it so that the students' parents will think the teacher is rigorous and the school has high academic standards. Extensive homework is frequently linked in our minds to high standards.

All of the factors described above play their part, but whether or not students are given homework, or even how much they are given, is not ultimately up to the individual teacher. Every teacher's work is directed by district policy, and most school districts have in place homework policies that mandate a specific homework time requirement per class. Homework policies are often drafted by the school board or by a special ad hoc committee. Composed of parents, teachers, and administrators, such committees are influenced by current teaching practice, community pressure, and national trends. Political rhetoric, too, can inflate expectations for homework levels—which explains, at least in part, some teacher's assertations that they favor homework because the public demands it.

"OUR KIDS ARE LAGGING BEHIND"

The twin drives for higher academic standards and increased parent involvement demand that more homework be given and that it be of a different quality.

Professor Martin Covington of the University of California at Berkeley questions the emphasis on elevated academic standards. He suggests that the call for more homework may be seen as an aspect of the "intensification movement," which postulates that education can be improved if there is just more *of* it—that is, more time in school, more homework, and more tests. He argues that "the fundamental problems that vex American education will not be relieved simply by increasing standards. Nor can we any longer afford the kinds of cheap rhetoric that reinvent higher standards from time to time for political gain."[17]

The current push for tougher academic standards is exemplified by a 1996 National Education Summit policy statement calling for higher expectations and standards and a broader use of technology.[18] Although there is ample evidence that high expectations on the part of parents and teachers can have a long-term positive effect on student performance, a different motive seems to be in play here: the calls for higher academic standards are most often heard in the context of American students' apparent *lack* of success in comparison to students elsewhere in the world. Such rhetoric has been especially pronounced in an era when American jobs have been lost to our international competitors; evidently it is far easier to blame students and schools than to consider that the fault may lie with inferior business practices or the new rules of the "global economy." Governor Bob Miller of Nevada joined the parade at the 1996 National Education Summit with his familiar assertion that "French, German and Japanese children aren't smarter than American children. They simply have greater expectations placed on them."[19]

Citing the low test scores of American students has become a favorite cocktail party game. However, some scholars have offered a more nuanced explanation for the poor showing by U.S. students in international academic performance comparisons, suggesting that it may have more to do with high levels of childhood poverty and a lack of support for families in the United States than with low academic standards, shorter school days, and fewer hours spent on homework. In 1991, 21.5 percent of American children under the age of eighteen belonged to families living below the poverty line, a figure that was the highest among a group of nineteen industrialized nations. The United States also had the second greatest gap between rich and poor, and was sixteenth in living standards for the poorest 20 percent of children. In addition, of these nineteen nations, the United States had the highest percentage of low-birth-weight children.[20] Of eight industrialized countries, the United States had the highest percentage of single-parent families.[21]

There appears to be a particular and consistent link between poverty rates and other family-structure variables and student performance on international math assessments. One study found that "achievement differences emerging from international comparisons might be at least partly attributable to differences in the social conditions experienced by children and youths growing up in these countries."[22] Unfortunately, as many educators have pointed out, the push for higher standards has diverted our attention from the real—or at the very least equally plausible—causes of academic failure: poverty and underfunded public schools.[23] Two major indicators of academic success are the mother's level of schooling and the socioeconomic status of the child.[24] Therefore, if we really wanted to boost academic achievement, we would see to it that all women in this country had at least a high school education and that no families lived in poverty. Increasing homework is a much cheaper policy, but the correlations and analysis that support it are far narrower than the domestic and cross-cultural research connecting inequality and lack of educational opportunity with poor student performance.

When educational leaders continue to cling to the traditional bromide of blaming students' lack of success on laziness, even in the face of other reasonable explanations, we must begin to suspect that the emphasis on homework serves the needs of powerful groups within our society. It is a sacred cow because it fits the ideological requirements of those who would maintain the status quo in our economy and politics. Sadly, teachers are often the ones who must implement policy that is designed at the local level but driven by national agendas and political trends. But was it always so?

CHAPTER 3

Homework in Historical Perspective

> No pupil under the age of fifteen years in any grammar or primary
> school shall be required to do any home study.
>
> California Civil Code, 1901[1]

Although homework may seem inevitable to us, belief in its benefits waxed and waned over the course of the twentieth century.
The importance our society attaches to homework and the arguments used to perpetuate it are tied to particular historical periods.
For at least the last two decades we have been in a "homework-is-
good-for-the-child-and-the-nation," period, so it may come as a
surprise to many of us that Americans have not always worshiped
homework.

THE NINETEENTH CENTURY

Scholars don't know much about the details of daily primary
school life and homework in the early nineteenth century. Historians have been unable to piece together a coherent picture of
how much time children spent on homework, the content of
that homework, or the role parents played in that work. They
have, however, established that student attendance in the primary
grades was unpredictable and the school year was short. Rural
teachers faced the challenge of single-handedly teaching all subjects to students whose ages ranged from six to twenty. In urban
areas, classrooms were crowded and understaffed. Education focused on reading, writing, and arithmetic, with reading lessons'
often doubling as instruction in morality and character building.

  When they reached grade five, large numbers of students left school for work. Beyond that point, the content and rigor of schooling changed considerably.[2] In these early grammar schools —our fifth through eighth grades—students studied history, geography, literature, and math. Discipline was harsh, and grading more stringent. "Learning" consisted of drill, memorization, and recitation. The memorization tasks were so imposing that parents had to promise to see to it that their children spent hours each night doing homework, at the expense of chores and other family obligations.

Only a very small percentage of students continued on to high school after grammar school. Those who did spent between two and three hours at home preparing for the daily recitation that was expected of them at school. Most historians agree that the students' parents had to make considerable sacrifices to provide the space and time necessary for their children to complete this homework. Even harder, perhaps, was the loss of potential family income, as their further schooling precluded these students from taking one of the many jobs available to those with a grammar school education.

If the preindustrial household of the early nineteenth century did not always require the long, hard hours of physical labor described by modern capitalism's defenders, it surely demanded fairly regular participation by all members of the family. Ivan Illich's classic depiction makes it clear why extended public schooling, in this era, was both less feasible and less necessary:

> In 1810, the common productive unit in New England was still the rural household. Processing and preserving of food, candlemaking, soapmaking, spinning, weaving, shoemaking, quilting, rugmaking, the keeping of small animals and gardens, all took place on domestic premises. . . . Women were as active in the creation of domestic self-sufficiency as were men.[3]

Needless to say, children played a very large role in this work, serving as apprentices in all these tasks in the expectation that they would one day assume responsibility for the household. Participation in the production of household goods and coordination of duties thus comprised a large part of the child's practical education.

By the late nineteenth century, a majority of Americans had migrated from farm to city, and many worked very long hours in factories. Children, too, were caught up in the cycle: with the parents strapped for both time and money, the labor of the child, either in the home or in the workplace, was often desperately needed.

Family life now centered on work. For many immigrants from preindustrial cultures, school offered an effective means of disciplining students to the long working hours of an expanding market economy. But whether because school detracted from the time available for household labor or because it carried an implicit message regarding industrial work that some immigrant parents didn't want to hear, the relationship between school and many working-class parents was conflictive. As today, parents undoubtedly complained about all the work their children were asked to do at school. The parents of a hundred years ago also believed that homework caused illness because students did not have enough chance to play in fresh air and sunshine, both thought to be vital to good health.

Occasionally, during this period, campaigns were mounted to limit homework. Concerns about the health risks of overstudy led some schools to curtail homework or abolish it altogether,[4] often over the objections of school principals, who reasoned that since parents were not required to send their children to school, those who wished to do so must be willing to abide by the school's rules. They argued that homework was not harmful to health and that it was an essential pedagogical tool. Given that drill, memorization, and recitation were thought to be the essence of education, these administrators no doubt felt justified in their conviction that students must spend long hours memorizing passages at home. Lacking broad-based support from school personnel, the anti-homework movements of the nineteenth century had little long-lasting effect.

By the end of the century, however, public sentiment had begun to change, and the pressure on the schools to abolish homework began to grow. Homework was now on the national agenda. As early as the 1880s, the president of the Boston school board, Francis A. Walker, a widely respected Civil War hero, had strongly criticized the practice:

> Over and over again have I had to send my own children, in spite of their tears and remonstrances, to bed, long after the assigned tasks had ceased to have any educational value and had become the means of nervous exhaustion and agitation, highly prejudicial to body and to mind; and I have no reason to doubt that such has been the experience of a large proportion of the parents whose children are habitually assigned home lessons in arithmetic.[5]

Antihomework sentiment in the nineteenth century focused on two key issues. One was the question of whether there was in fact any educational value in homework. The other was homework's perceived threat to the physical, emotional, and mental health of the child. For advocates of children's emotional health, even arguments in favor of homework's supposed educational value were outweighed by the prospects of its long-term detriment to the child.

The turn-of-the-century antihomework crusade would become a centerpiece in the agenda of the progressive education movement of the twentieth century. Educational leaders would begin to question the very structure of teaching in the schools. And once the value of drill, memorization, and recitation was opened to debate, the attendant need for homework came under harsh scrutiny as well.[6]

THE FIRST HALF OF THE TWENTIETH CENTURY: HEALTH AND HAPPINESS

It's tempting, when reading about the homework debates in the early years of the twentieth century, to imagine what it must have been like to live then. Certainly cause and effect *seemed* much clearer. If you took your daughter to the eye doctor for glasses, for example, he might well send a note to school advising that she be given no more homework because it was bad for her eyes. Instead of being given Ritalin, your ten-year-old son might be instructed to get 7 hours of vigorous physical exercise . . . as much as possible *before* school each day. And rather than labeling your child ADHD, the doctor might testify at a school board meeting that homework was causing him or her to develop a nervous condition.

Or again, if we lived in 1934, we might think that the acne we now take as a sign of adolescence was really due to a lack of fresh air and sunshine—caused by homework! We could read numerous editorials stating that the root of violence in the schools was the stress of kids' working too many hours, and homework would be named as the culprit.

Even as educational leaders began to question the practice within their own circles, parents who struggled with their children over homework could find solace in the writings of Edward Bok, the editor of the *Ladies' Home Journal*. His January 1900 article, "A National Crime at the Feet of American Parents," became a rallying cry for the antihomework forces.[7] Arguing that homework posed grave health risks for children, he cited lack of sunshine and fresh air as a leading cause of the nervous disorders from which thousands of young people then suffered. He pointed out that schooling had changed so much over the previous decade that most parents were unable to help their children with schoolwork. Asserting that in any case, "five hours a day of brain work was the most we should ask of our children,"[8] he called for homework to be abolished entirely for those under fifteen and limited to an hour a night for older students. He urged parents to take the lead in working more closely with the schools, and to demand that new limits be set on homework.

In a series of *Ladies' Home Journal* articles, Bok continued to build his case: homework was an intrusion into family life, he insisted, and interfered with the rights of both children and parents.[9] A number of physicians soon joined the battle, protesting forcefully about the health risks of homework.

Bok's writing helped galvanize a more widespread movement; by 1930 a Society for the Abolition of Homework had been organized. By then, progressive ideas had taken hold in education.[10] Increasingly, schools were viewed as the workplace of the young, and in the best progressive tradition, these workplaces were often seen as being in need of reforms that would guarantee humane conditions for workers. The role of the expert was paramount: the work of the school must be done *in* the school, under the watchful eye of a trained teacher and in an environment specially designed for learning. Educators came to see the educational importance of proper lighting, desks of adequate size and shape, and quiet spaces. Most homes, lacking such amenities, were judged to be ill suited for study.[11]

In a smaller battle of the national war being waged by labor leaders over working conditions and work hours, homework was attacked as an illicit extension of the working day by those who viewed schoolwork as labor. These critics wanted to apply the newly defined child labor laws to schoolwork; to them, homework was work and should be regulated as such.[12]

By and large, however, it was the health risks of homework that caused the greatest concern. Homework was blamed for eyestrain, stress, lack of sleep, and even physical deformity. In a 1935 letter to the *New York Times,* one writer claimed, "Homework is directly responsible for more undernourished, nervous, bespectacled, round-shouldered children than you can possibly imagine."[13] Part and parcel of the health argument against homework was the charge that it deprived children of an important element of childhood: play. Just as some psychologists and labor advocates in the twenties and thirties cited the role of recreation in human development in their campaigns to shorten the work week, educational reformers argued that play was an integral part of the development of the child. Homework was seen as limiting the child's ability to develop certain skills and attitudes that could be learned only when he or she was free to play. One educator claimed that ten-year-old children needed six or seven hours of vigorous physical activity daily.[14]

Belief in the benefits of fresh air and sunshine was so widespread that in 1912 the Ethical Culture School in New York City established its own Open Air Department, a "roof school" designed to meet the demand for open-air education. Directed by Miss Bessie Stillman and Miss Anna Gillinghans, the school psychologist, the Open Air Department provided a rooftop educational setting complete with movable walls, windows, and desks. The classroom was often transformed into a playground as students flowed smoothly from academic work to rigorous outdoor play. Students were supplied with "sitting-out bags" with large hoods and gloves to protect them from the elements. An "announcement" from the Ethical Culture School archives boasts, "It has been remarked that 'nervous' habits observable in every ordinary class-room, choreic symptoms and the like, are unusually rare among the Roof classes."[15]

The Open Air Department also proved valuable as an experimental station where school personnel could try out various forms of grading, group projects, study skills programs, and integrated arts and crafts. Perhaps the most notable innovation was the elimination of assigned homework, about which administrators observed:

> Few results have been more gratifying than the children's attitude towards home work. Unless a child is temporarily or permanently behind his class on the one hand or on the other hand is working definitely to enter a higher grade, no home work is permitted in the fifth or sixth grades without the special request of the parents. . . . For a long time the Ethical Culture School has believed that there is grave danger lest home work be done in such a manner as to weaken children intellectually and foster poor habits of study. Indeed too much home help and emphasis upon results for a daily assignment may even afford training in actual dishonesty. . . . The omission of required homework made possible by the longer school day, as well as the fresh air and breaks in the routine for vigorous exercise, [account for the fact] that the children have improved in health, and that in some cases there has been marked increase in alertness and mental grasp.[16]

The Open Air Department closed in 1928, when the Fieldston School opened and the roof was transformed into a much-needed playground. Robert Rothschild, an Open Air alumnus, still remembers the excitement of being fitted for the "sitting-out bags," and the sense of adventure the program fostered. He attributes his lifelong ruggedness and self-reliance to the influence of school's methods and philosophy, the way manual labor and mental labor flowed smoothly one into another, and the emphasis on the importance of hardiness.[17]

In the world beyond the Open Air experiment, even as homework's critics charged that it intruded on the rights of families and that it was unhealthy, the question of its academic value remained unresolved among educators. Part of the problem consisted in the very definition of learning. In the nineteenth century the mind had been viewed as a large muscle that needed to be developed, most usefully through memorization. Implicit in this view, of course, was the belief that the mind was a blank slate ready to receive impressions from the world, and the child, by extension, a passive recipient of information.

In the first half of the twentieth century, our thinking about the mind evolved. Mind was now viewed as the great evolutionary achievement of humans: just as the spots on a leopard enabled it to survive in nature, so did human survival depend on the use of the mind to solve problems. Learning thus came to be seen as an active process of problem solving.[18]

Hours of memorization at home did not fit into this definition of learning. The notion of the mind as a problem-solving device has become a commonplace in educational thinking today, but the questions of how to define learning and how to measure it remain at the heart of the debate that still rages about the value of homework.

THE SECOND HALF OF THE TWENTIETH CENTURY: HOMEWORK GROWS UP

Not long past the halfway point of the twentieth century, a critical historical event served as a catalyst for a renewed effort to intensify homework. With the 1957 launch of *Sputnik*, the Russians "beat" us into space and permanently changed the American educational landscape. The fifty-year trend toward less homework came to a sudden end when the country became obsessed with competing with the Russians; by 1961 the vast majority of educators and parents professed themselves in favor of more homework.

Coming as it did just a year after the launch of *Sputnik*, the National Defense Education Act (NDEA) sought to improve math and science education. It provided loans to undergraduates and fellowships to graduate students; at the institutional level, it sought to overhaul guidance and testing services and to revise and strengthen curricula. Requiring students to do more math homework was a major cultural and curricular objective.

At the time, of course, this emphasis on more math and science at home and in school seemed to be an appropriate response to an international emergency. But at forty years' remove, the linking of *Sputnik* as military threat to educational reforms as appropriate response merits closer scrutiny.

Surely Russia's continued development of missiles and satellite technologies constituted a potential long-term threat to the United States. But by many other indicators of military might cited by conventional authorities, the United States was universally deemed to be superior.[19] Why, then, did so many political and media leaders become fixated on this event?

By portraying *Sputnik* and the "collectivist" economic system that produced it as both able and poised to destroy us, business and political leaders managed to reaffirm and rally support for traditional values of individual initiative, hard work, corporate enterprise, and technological advance. If we all worked hard enough in our schools, labs, and workplaces, the message was, we could achieve far more success than the Soviets, and set an example that the Third World would admire. But first we needed to provide educational opportunities and challenges for everyone, and put racial divisiveness behind us so the rest of the world would embrace our values.

In this regard, our leaders reflected and reinforced a mindset that went all the way back to the Puritans. Our nation is "a city upon a hill," and as such, its values and guiding institutions can be proved worthy only if, and only to the extent that, others are found wanting. In such a context, only conquest or conversion of those who are different can be appropriate. Even for ourselves, commitment must be total, and it must begin at a young age.

Sputnik as proof of a different and threatening economic system carried questionable assumptions and ultimately took a heavy toll. The focus on more math and science as the key to our economic and military success against an implacable foe helped obscure other areas of domestic tension and insecurity. If NDEA succeeded in improving math and science learning in schools and homes, would our business and government leaders make the best use of the newly trained students? Or were there other demands implicit in our business and consumer culture that led some students here and many more abroad to resist the "American way of life?" Even if the United States were to retain and enhance its status as the predominant military and economic power, would that example itself be sufficient to carry all else before it? And was unanimity of purposes and life styles really a necessary prerequisite for the U.S. to retain the allegiance of its citizens and its ability to survive?

By the sixties, homework had come to be seen as a primary means of increasing academic achievement, even though the research to support this claim was problematic. In reaction to the increased attention being paid to the role of homework, a new homework debate was launched in the late sixties and the seventies, echoing the concerns raised in the early part of the century. Once again, the debate reflected and reinforced other concerns about the whole political economy. As such late-sixties classics as Studs Terkel's *Working* documented, many American workers, not simply disaffected college students, worried about the pace and length of the working day as well as the quality of life in the workplace.

In much the same vein, newspapers and women's magazines suggested that children were too tired to do homework. Parents argued that children worked a full day at school and should, like any workers, be free at night to engage in leisure-time activities; as it was, homework disrupted family life and caused tensions between parents and their children. Some felt that homework reduced children's interest in and enthusiasm for school, while others voiced concern that homes were not conducive to study and that homework stunted development. This time around, mental health workers raised the subject of suicide and questioned whether school pressure might be part of the problem. A statement published by the American Educational Research Association emphasized this aspect:

> For mental health, children and young people need to engage in worthwhile out-of-school tasks suited to their individual capacities. Homework should supply such tasks and reasonable freedom in carrying them out. Whenever homework crowds out social experience, outdoor recreation, and creative activities, and whenever it usurps time that should be devoted to sleep, it is not meeting the basic needs of children and adolescents.[20]

The National Education Association took up the cause and issued its own statement in 1966:

> It is generally recommended (a) that children in the early elementary school period have no homework specifically assigned by the teacher; (b) that limited amounts of homework—not more than an hour a day—be introduced during the upper elementary school and junior high years; (c) that homework be limited to four nights a week; and (d) that in secondary school no more than one and a half hours a night be expected. If the weekends and one evening in the middle of the week are left free, the pupil has the opportunity to develop appreciation and skill in art and music and participate more fully in the social life of the family and community. The trend, theoretically at least, is toward homework that is optional, creative, and recreational.[21]

These recommendations, it goes without saying, were ignored by school administrators and policymakers.

The battle over homework was at its most intense during the thirties and sixties, two progressive periods in our political and educational history. Furthermore, these progressive currents in educational discourse resonated with other contemporaneous debates. Labor leaders, cultural critics, and reformers alike questioned whether the amount of time spent on homework or in factory work was detrimental to the physical health and creativity of the student or worker. Today many educators dismiss these two eras in educational history as romantic or sentimental; in this they unwittingly mirror mainstream business and political leaders resistant to economic reform of any kind.

Progressive educators believed that schools needed to educate the whole child, and that a happy, joyful child was an essential condition for education. The children's parents were windfall beneficiaries of these progressive beliefs: homework was seen as unfair to them, since they worked hard all day and deserved some rest and relaxation at home without the strain of helping with their children's schoolwork.

HOMEWORK AND A "NATION AT RISK"

As the United States entered the eighties, education reform was once again a key theme. As in the post-*Sputnik* era, the language was one of foreign challenge, and the rhetoric was militaristic. But now the terrain was the economy, and the perceived threat was the loss of the nation's capacity for economic survival. *A Nation at Risk* merits detailed analysis today for several reasons. In a recent cover story on homework, Time magazine characterized that 1983 report as the publication that "racheted up the pressure to get tough again" on homework.[22] But the document was much more. It was the first major report by the government attempting to prove that the purported inadequacies of our schools and our students were responsible for the troubles of the U.S. economy. In addition, its portrayal of foreign economies as not only different from but bent on our economic destruction set the tone for much of the "competitiveness" debate today. Finally, as the *Time* article itself illustrates, this study remains even today the canonical text for many who seek to blame students and teachers for continuing national problems.[23]

The authors of the report suggested:

> Our nation is at risk. Our once unchallenged preeminence in commerce, industry, science, and technological innovation is being over-

taken by competitors throughout the world. . . . If an unfriendly power had attempted to impose on America the mediocre educational performance that exists today, we might well have viewed it as an act of war.[24]

In the course of a general commentary on the state of U.S. education, the authors proceeded to emphasize the need for higher standards in math, science, English, and foreign-language instruction. They complained that homework had been reduced and argued that students should do more homework and have a much longer school year.

Ostensibly, the tone and recommendations of this document can be attributed to the economic success being enjoyed at the time by the Japanese. The United States was experiencing not only relatively slow economic growth but a burgeoning trade deficit with Japan. Nonetheless, just as the backdrop for *Sputnik* had been a set of doubts and conflicts over economic competitiveness, racial justice, and the role of the United States in a postcolonial world, *A Nation at Risk* had late-seventies concerns and anxieties as its subtext.

For many Americans, the dream of economic growth as the key to the good life was offset by concerns that unlimited growth might do irreparable damage to the planet. For others, the relentless emphasis on work and consumption disrupted family life and eroded leisure time. These implicit challenges to or anxieties regarding central values were, however, hardly acknowledged in *A Nation at Risk*. Not only was the ethic of individual initiative, hard work, and production portrayed as essential to our survival, but other nations with divergent values and practices were depicted as uniquely bent on our destruction and willing to stop at nothing to achieve that end. Thus Japanese practices of subsidizing strategic industries merited a brief note, but no mention was made of the role that subsidies and tariffs played in America's own economic development. Foreign economic systems were characterized as completely different from ours and utterly hostile to us:

History is not kind to idlers. The time is long past when American destiny was assured simply by an abundance of inexhaustible human enthusiasm and by our relative isolation from the malignant problems of older civilizations. The world is indeed one global village. We live among determined, well-educated, and strongly motivated competitors. We compete with them for international standing and markets, not only with products but with the ideas of our laboratories and neighborhood workshops. America's position in the world may once have been reasonably secure with only a few exceptionally well trained men and women. It is no longer.[25]

Once again, as had been the case in the *Sputnik* controversy, the authors of *A Nation at Risk* left unexamined the role that a number of established American institutions may have played in whatever economic dislocations were being experienced. Jobs were being "lost" to Japanese competitors, but what of the American firms that "moved" those jobs or totally relocated? Education was portrayed as a vehicle for establishing and reinforcing common values, but why could it not equally challenge received wisdom or redress social inequities? Finally, in language that has become virtually canonical today, the globalization of commerce and the "global village" were taken simply as givens, but what about the political, institutional, and technological choices that went into their creation?

In such a context, it is hardly surprising that the authors endorsed longer homework hours. It fits well with established notions of individualism and with an emphasis on work as the central feature of life. Moreover, it provides some good early training in respecting authority, and may ease the way to acceptance of the opportunities and roles that most workers actually have in major U.S. corporations.

The push for homework has waxed and waned over the last two centuries. It is possible to make a case for homework as a necessary and salutary response to external demands upon our political economy; from such a perspective, it would be unexceptional, like the kind of training a marathon runner must do to meet the biological challenge of running the race. But societies are more than biological organisms, and external events are not only understood but even recognized exclusively though categories that help us make sense of our experience.

To the extent that our leaders are bent on confirming their view of work, economic growth, individual initiative, and market economies as not merely a reasonable way to organize life but the *only* way, they are likely to dismiss gripes about homework as little more than the loneliness of the long-distance runner. But if there are reasons to doubt both the centrality and the all-inclusive nature of such values, then homework is surely worth a second look.

Homework is now on center stage once again. The challenge posed, whether militarily or ideologically, by the Soviets has been replaced by the more diffuse but equally problematic rhetoric of global trade wars. By the nineties, politicians were calling on Congress to mandate more homework. In his 1994 State of the Union address, Bill Clinton encouraged parents to help their children with . . . their homework. Hotlines, Internet nodes, and high-priced tutors have proliferated to meet the increasing demands of homework. It has once again been integrated into debates about work and, more broadly, the very sanctity of our way of life. But like their predecessors in the thirties and the sixties, homework's current proponents clearly have business and political agendas, and a vested interest in imparting and defending their own views of the political economy.

Parents of school-age children need not be reminded of how much homework they are expected to do these days. The recommended limit of thirty years ago—one and a half hours a night for high school students—now seems like a dream. Just as businesses stretch parents' working hours with abandon, schools feel no compunction about adding homework. We read the accounts from the thirties and can barely imagine that it could ever have been OK to say that kids needed downtime from schoolwork.

We are led to wonder, has medical science proved that kids do not really need fresh air and sunshine? Can the mental-health profession assure us that there is no harm in kids' driving themselves in school all day and then doing hours of homework well into the night?

At the simplest level, our reading of this history convinces us that neither our children's education nor the larger culture will suffer if reasonable limits are placed on the independent work expected of students outside the classroom. We also believe that assistance for such work should be provided within a school setting, not at home.

We base our case not only on pedagogical grounds but on some fundamental understanding of the limits of our political economy as well. Our pedagogical argument contends that both research and historical experience fail to demonstrate the necessity or efficacy of ever longer hours of homework.

At the level of political economy, we believe that reforms in homework practices are central to a politics of family and personal liberation. Work and homework are among our core values and assume a significant role in our lives, but they do not define the totality of those lives. It is entirely legitimate and appropriate periodically to question the extent to which even core values should dominate our lives. In the twenties and thirties, debate about such issues as the length of the standard workweek elicited an outcry from business leaders that any reduction in work hours would make American capitalism unsustainable, and possibly even lead to social anarchy. Yet the capitalism that emerged after World War II managed to reconcile a shortening of hours with the most sustained productivity increases in our history.

Unquestioned acceptance of the intensity or extent of core values, as has been the rule in this society since the late sixties, is hardly the way to affirm them. Such a politics of denial must lead eventually either to the quiet subversion of those values or even to their indiscriminate destruction.

The parents and teachers who are beginning to question the value of more and more homework may defy conventional wisdom, but in this they have many ancestors. As we have seen, America has a long history of skepticism regarding the pedagogical value of homework, and a tradition of examining the price children and families must pay for the practice. We would do well to continue that history and that tradition as a new century begins.

CHAPTER 4

Kids and Homework

Distress over homework has been cited as one of the reasons for
a recent spate of suicides among schoolchildren, some of whom
have been as young as nine. As a result, Hong Kong is seen as one
of the worst countries in the industrialised world for primary
school stress.

The *Harare* [Zimbabwe] *Herald*, October 26, 1997[1]

For all that researchers may quibble over the validity of their findings about it and educators may try to devise innovative ways to
approach it, it is, after all, the kids who actually have to *do* homework. So what do they think of it, and why do they so often refuse
to do it? In the past, researchers rarely went to the students themselves to get information; like laboratory rats, they were acted
upon, rather than being active agents in the research process.
More recently, however, we have begun to hear from students
about their schooling experiences.

If we can concede that human beings are more than rats in a
maze and that their actions can be neither explained nor even
comprehended without some understanding of the concepts and
ideas expressed in their actions, then we need to let the students
talk to us if we want to have any real sense the role of homework
in their lives. The recent rise in so-called ethnographic research
within the schools has allowed us to undertake such a task.

The inclusion of student narratives in analysis lends a depth of
detail to research findings that is necessarily missing from large-
scale studies. Some researchers have gone so far as to suggest, in
fact, that trying to piece together *why* students don't do their

homework is much more important than tracking questionable correlations between, for example, reported homework time and academic achievement.

EXCUSES OR REASONS

In one study of students' reasons for failing to complete homework, Pat Hinchey received some unsurprising responses. Nonetheless, she was impressed by the logic and persuasiveness of the students' voices. The number-one reason students gave for not doing their homework was that they didn't have enough time. Students reported that they needed a social life and didn't do their homework because, by one typical account,

> some of my girlfriends tell me that they're skipping homework because they want to spend time with their boyfriends or hang out with their friends. Sometimes I don't do my homework because I need to get out of the house, go to parties, have guests coming over, have clothes to wash, have friends to help with advice, songs to record from the radio.[2]

As Hinchey points out, we usually respond to this line of reasoning by telling our children that school is their job and that it must be given first priority. "Work before play" is a constant theme in our culture, and in most households, homework is viewed as the work of the child. But should it be, really? Many developmental psychologists would argue instead that the first priority for adolescents is developing a social self.[3] Adolescence is a time when a new self is emerging, with all the attendant chaos implied by that transformation. Learning to manage that self amid the demands of the world is an essential part of the maturing process. Denying the reality of new and competing goals and emotions by chaining the self to the idealized and even intensified standards of the adult workplace not only fails to contribute to maturation, but is a sure route to rebellion or extreme distress—if not immediately, then often later in life. In the response quoted above, the student talks about the other things she *needs* to do, most of which have to do with social relations. Most developmental psychologists would agree that working out such relations is the adolescent's primary task.[4]

We have come to accept the notion that education must be developmentally appropriate. Children are not asked to learn to read until they are five because we believe they are not *ready* to read before that age. Unfortunately, most of us don't apply the same logic to older students. How often have we told our children they can't talk to their friends until their homework is done? But the real work of adolescence is learning how to relate to others socially.

Hinchey suggests that schoolwork is properly the work of teachers. Some teachers may take weeks to return tests to students, which leads Hinchey to wonder if homework is really *their* top priority.[5] Usually teachers respond to students' queries about their unreturned tests with vague promises such as, "I'll have them to you next week." Imagine if a student said, "Sorry, I didn't get to study for the test, I'll take it next week"! This analogy is not meant to imply that teachers should spend all their evenings grading papers rather than being with their families and friends; but it may be helpful to realize that often teachers do not do their own homework. Teachers are not evaluated on the work they are expected to do after hours, such as how quickly they return papers or how thoroughly they grade tests. Yet it is common for parents to be told that their child's grade was low because of "incomplete homework."

Another reason students give for not doing homework is that they have other responsibilities.

> The average student is involved in after-school activities. In our school, homework averages about three hours a night. Some students play baseball, basketball, football, which lasts until 6:00. Then to get home on the train is another two and a half hours for some students. DINNER IS IN THERE SOMEWHERE, and it's not healthy to go to sleep every night at two A.M.! Where's the time?[6]

We all want our children to be well rounded, to have a wide variety of activities that capture their imagination and spark their passion. But are students in training for a life that is not their own?

Because many of us have accepted that we must work twelve-hour days, we may not notice that our children are working that long as well. Or when we do notice it, we may assuage any doubts about our own very stressed lives by telling ourselves and our children that this is the way the world is, and they'd better get used to it now.

A third reason students gave Hinchey for not doing homework was that there was no point in doing it. Students claimed that teachers didn't collect it and that it didn't have anything to do with what they were being tested on in class. Students who were in academic trouble reported that they were so far behind that it didn't matter anymore—they would never "get it." "Maybe you are not good at that subject and it just doesn't matter how much help you get, you still can't do it," one such student explained. "You just think you'll fail no matter what."[7]

From the other end of the academic spectrum, Hinchey heard a different sort of "there's-no-point":

> If you think you know the subject really well, and if you think the homework is really simple and not needed, then you probably won't do it. Some students are innately intelligent to the point where, if they hear something once, they remember it. Therefore they can average a 90 on exams without doing homework or studying.[8]

In sum, Hinchey cautions, "It's time to stop dismissing students' criticisms as irrelevant excuses for laziness, to ask ourselves if we deserve their criticism, and to start thinking critically about exactly what we assign, under what conditions, and why."[9]

As parents, we have all heard this before, from our own children. Sadly, most of us just press them harder and harder to complete their homework. But as Hinchey suggests, embedded in the voices of the children are real needs that have to be met and issues that we must address.

One of us (Etta) conducted interviews with high school dropouts as part of a study for the Maine Department of Education. During the interviews, she asked her sujects if there was a moment when they knew they were going to drop out of school. Their responses included tales of incomplete homework and the inability to fit homework into their lives. Taken together, these stories drove home for us the fact that for many students, homework is more of a hindrance than a help.

> The teacher yells and screams at everyone and kicks the trash can because the kids didn't do their homework. It's hard to do homework when you have a baby to take care of. Once he had a fit and I had a fit. . . .
>
> —Sally, 16, Dexter, Maine

> I got detention because you [sic] supposed to have your parent sign your homework and I forged mine 'cause my parents work at night and the teacher knew it was forged and I had a really bad day so I sort of cleared her desk and she sent me to the office. I knew then [in sixth grade] that school wasn't for me.
>
> —Matt, 15, Bar Harbor, Maine

> I knew I wasn't going to make it my junior year. I was in for two months and doin' allright but then I got behind in my homework and couldn't catch up. I was too embarrassed to ask for help, so it's my fault, I can't blame them.
>
> —Tray, 17, Fairfield, Maine

> One day the teacher said I was worthless because I didn't do my homework. I hit him and drove his teeth into his tongue. I'm just pissed I didn't hit him harder. I just don't like being told what to do all the time, like I'm an anarchist but they [the school] control my day and my night.
>
> —David, 16, Dexter, Maine

These student comments raise all sorts of questions that we rarely think about. When students say they can't finish their homework, why do teachers assume they are lying or just giving them rationalizations? Does it occur to the teachers to ask the students *why* they didn't do their homework? Is a person worthless if he or she fails to do homework?

There is of course a long tradition, going back at least as far as Plato, of lamenting that youth is going astray, and predicting that if the young don't live by the standards of adult society, they will pull that society down, either now or later, when they come to assume the responsibilities of adulthood. Yet as one reviews even the most recent such rounds of rhetoric, one cannot help being struck by how exaggerated the claims seem. Perhaps we should consider the possibility that our reactions to the excesses and lack of discipline of the young may reflect our own doubts and insecurities about the demands we are making on our children and ourselves.

HOMEWORK CASE STUDY:
AN ISLAND IN NEW ENGLAND

One of us (Etta again) taught a college-prep philosophy course at the local high school as part of a college/school district teacher exchange. To practice our principles, no homework was given in this class. The students and their parents were told that because philosophy was so difficult to read, we would be doing all the reading in class. In addition, parents were informed that all writing would be done in class as well. This would ensure that the students did their own thinking about the material and their own work. The parents were a bit skeptical, but since the class was experimental to begin with, they agreed. We read philosophy out loud in class, in small groups, as a whole class, and to each other in reading groups. Students debated the meanings, discussed the issues, and pondered the implications of the texts for their own lives. Since all the reading and writing was done in class, it was obvious what students were struggling with and what was easy for them. Misconceptions could be cleared up quickly. There was a fairness about the in-class writing precisely because parents weren't there to help. The students couldn't call their friends for explanations help or copy random paragraphs out of old encyclopedias. At the end of the semester, I asked the class to write about the experience of not having homework. The following is a sampling of the responses.

> I cannot even begin to tell you how much I love not having homework! You know, the weird thing is that we don't have any additional outside work, yet I feel like I actually think more. I really like work-

ing entirely in class because there are always people to converse with if you have questions and other people contribute ideas that you might otherwise not think of. Also, since I'm a senior I have so much work to do, like filling out applications and visiting colleges, that the less homework I have, the easier my life is.

This student reminds us of the social dimension of learning. She was happy to receive as much input as possible in her thinking on a particular topic. She acknowledged the importance of listening to others' points of view and learned to be a team player in the process of not having homework. She found that other people's ideas had merit and could contribute to her own understanding.

No homework is good because philosophy cannot be read in front of the television or read in your bedroom right before you go to bed. It must be read in pairs and discussed to gain the full effect of what the author is trying to get you to understand.

We know where this student habitually did his homework! But he wasn't happy with the status quo, and his desire to understand what he was learning came through in his comments. Reading took on new meaning for him as a result of this experience. Like others, he came to see the social dimension of learning and to value its role in his own education.

No homework is great—less worries going into class. Let's us have freedom to think our way in the class. Not having homework is great! I can concentrate fully on philosophy while I'm in here without the niggling worry about whether or not my homework is done.

These students' words hint at the stress that high school students are under. Many students spoke about not worrying about homework when they were in this class. I hadn't realized that students often sat in other classes and spent the whole period worrying that they might be called upon to recite from homework they hadn't completed. It is hard to calculate just how much stress homework creates in students, but if the suicide report that opens this chapter is any indication, it may be a considerable amount.

> I agree so much with your theory on homework. Why give it? I believe that any essay that I write in this class is going to be so much different (so much better) because I'm doing it when it's fresh in my mind and I'm not doing it in front of TV or during dinner. I'm not rushing to talk on the phone. I'm taking my time and doing a good job on it too. Also any homework some kids don't do would put them behind and it wouldn't be fair to their reading partner or their group. . . . So we're always all together and no one person is behind and not knowing what's going on in class.

This student's comments are perhaps the most telling of all in terms of our basic theme. They speak to the unevenness of classroom discussion in a conventional setting—that is, in a class with assigned homework. Some students will have done the homework and some not; the former will dominate the discussions, and the latter will try to hide their failure behind minimal participation and thus slow things down. This student's underlying expression of fairness should remind all of us that adolescents have a strong sense of justice, and that at least one adolescent could see the injustice of homework, which pits students who can against students who can't.

Indirectly, her comments also underscore just how closely connected the issue of homework is to broader questions of equality in American life. Those who assume that greater equality in our workplaces and communities is neither possible nor desirable are less likely to take this last student's concerns seriously. But perhaps this is another area in which the discontent of some youngsters with the present order deserves closer attention on the part of adults.

Earlier in this chapter we discussed the ways in which homework may in fact push some kids out of school. We heard ex-students say that their inability to complete homework caused them to drop out. The college-prep students in Etta's philosophy course had interesting insights of their own into the educational value of homework—or, in this instance, *no* homework. In their own way, these high-achieving students also struggled with the practice, but unlike the dropouts, they may feel the consequences or recognize the damage done only much later in life.

One young man who heard Etta speak about homework told her his story. A junior at Columbia, at the top of his class, he was struggling with social relations:

> You know, all I did in high school was homework. Sure I got in the ninety-ninth percentile on the SATs, but now I wish I had hung out with some friends or had a girlfriend. I don't even really know how to be someone's friend or how to meet someone. I really wasted a lot of time in high school doing homework. I would have been much better off getting Bs and being in the ninetieth percentile on the SATs; at least I might know how to have fun and hang out now. It's hard to learn in college.

Everyone has a homework story to tell. A news reporter who was doing a story on our position on homework told Etta he was having a hard time getting an angle. He couldn't find anyone in the schools who agreed with her, and he didn't know what else to do. Explaining that homework was perhaps best thought about from a personal point of view, she suggested that he review about his own experiences with homework, or his kids' experiences, and take the story from there. A few days later he called to say:

> I hadn't thought about this in a long time. I am a fifty-year-old man who has been a writer all my life. But as a student, I was a really bad writer. I used to hide my books in the woods on my way home from school and lie to my parents when they asked if I had any homework because I didn't want them to see how bad my writing was. It took me a long time to get over my shame at not being able to do well on my homework.

Policy analysis of homework, as of many other topics, is best done through close observation of those who are on the receiving end, rather than from the perspective of experts who wish to fit actual experience to preconceived notions. We need to take our lived reality as the starting point for our thinking about homework. We need to listen to our kids when they say they are sick and tired of school, or they just want to "veg," or they have to see their friends. Respecting their needs and honoring their voices should be our first priority in rethinking the homework wars. This poem by twelve-year-old Noah Mohr poem could serve as inspiration:

HOMEWORK
Homework this and homework that.
That's all I hear about
at home after school.
I mean what is up with it?
Who made it up?
If I ever find out,
S/he is going to get a letter
from me that they will not forget.
That is if they are still around.
I think homework is like mowing the lawn,
doing the dishes and cleaning your room.
Why, you ask?
Because you have someone telling you
what to do (teachers/parents).
Schoolwork is math, science, geography,
reading and English.
I'm not telling the teacher
to get rid of it.
I'm just saying
try to put it in a fun form.

His dad says Noah spends a "mind-boggling" amount of time on homework. His dad doesn't remember ever doing so much homework himself and wishes Noah had some time to just lie in a field and look at the clouds.

CHAPTER 5

Homework and the Level Playing Field

The students in my school are from blue-collar families, so of course their test scores are low.

Principal in a rural New England community

After the principal of a local elementary school was quoted in the newspaper as blaming blue-collar families for the low test scores of her students, townspeople were up in arms. Insulted, hurt, and convinced that she was simply making excuses for bad teaching, parents spoke among themselves about whether someone with "those views" should be leading "our school."

Sadly, the principal was right in one sense. Test scores *are* tied directly to the wealth of a community: the more money, the higher the test scores. Although Asian communities tend to fall a bit outside this very clear correlation, the social class/test score connection in the United States has been otherwise consistent since researchers first started comparing schools using students' standardized test scores as a measure in the early fifties.

The correlation between social class and academic achievement has been the subject of intense scholarly analysis throughout the past half century. Much of this research has, in turn, been implicated in major policy failures. The thrust of work has been to fashion an educational system that by virtue of either its curriculum or its support services can overcome the effects of unequal funding for our public schools—or, even more fundamentally, of the very unequal class structure in which those schools are situated. But all of these efforts share one problematic assumption—

namely, that schools by themselves can correct for the damage done by a highly inequitable class structure. Although schools may be able to play a role in such reform, asking them to do the whole job can often lead to counterproductive consequences.

As early as 1916, educators reported that "where the parents are illiterate or for other reasons are unable or unwilling to supervise the home study, their children as a rule either make slow progress or are failures entirely when measured by the progress of their companions in school."[1] Periodically over the last hundred years educators have tried to call attention to the ways in which homework assignments further handicap poor students, but their warnings have generally gone unheeded. Homework may just be one of those schooling practices, like tracking, that in fact serve to sort students according to class and to magnify the class differences inherent in our society.

HOMEWORK IN THE LIVES OF DIFFERENT CHILDREN

> Compare and contrast the domestic policies of FDR and Clinton.
>
> Homework assignment, U.S. history,
> 11th grade, rural New England high school

As Alix leaves school to return home to her trailer and her two-year-old daughter, she has every intention of doing the assignment for U.S. history. She gets home at 2:30 only to discover that her daughter has a fever of 103. Alix takes her to the closest medical center, forty miles from her home. By 5:30 she is back home nursing a sick child and getting dinner ready for her father and two brothers. By 7:15, with the baby finally asleep, Alix sits down in the room she shares with her baby to begin working. She finds that she has left her textbook at school. She calls a friend who drives her back to school, which is thirty minutes from her home. At 9:00 she gets a call from her best friend, whose father has beaten her again and who asks if she can spend the night at Alix's. Sue arrives at 10:00 and needs some comforting. . . .

David arrives home after tennis practice. His mother asks how his day was and if he has any tough homework. David tells her about the U.S. history assignment. As they eat, she talks to him about FDR and Clinton. In the course of the conversation, they discuss an appropriate thesis for his paper. David goes to his room and turns on his computer. He discovers that he has left his textbook at school. He goes downstairs to the family room to ask his dad about books that might be helpful to him. His dad begins to pull books off the family bookshelves: an encyclopedia, a book by Howard Zinn, and a Time-Life book about the thirties. David returns to his room and begins again.

These two stories, both factual, illustrate the full spectrum of hardships and opportunities faced by students in our society. Of course stories such as Alix's are also insights into the problems of uncaring teachers and teen pregnancy. Many high school dropouts in Etta's study for the State of Maine talked about the chaotic structure of their schools and the lack of support services offered. It would be foolish to assume that if homework had not been a part of the school bargain, these students would all have made it. But clearly, from the point of view of the students, homework compounded the difficulties thay had to cope with. This finding is confirmed by Harris Cooper, who noted that "homework may increase time-on-task for better students from better homes, but at the same time, for disadvantaged children, create frustrating situations that are detrimental to learning. In such cases, homework may contribute to a social ill, rather than help remedy it."[2]

When we talk about students from "better" homes, we are using the term in several ways. On the most obvious level, "better" refers to the wealth, and hence the physical facilities, available to students. It is far easier to complete one's homework when a quiet room, adequate lighting, computers, books, and other cultural resources are readily available. Only adding to the disparity is the fact that in most U.S. communities, budgets for libraries and other public facilities that might ease the impact of individual family differences have been greatly scaled back. In many communities, even the schools themselves are no longer open for as many after-school hours as they once were. The fiscal crisis of the public sector has had an especially adverse impact on the burdens shouldered by poor and working-class students.

The notion of "better" families carries other implications as well. The nature of an adult's employment—whether on an assembly line, as an office secretary, as a mid- or upper-level manager, or as an independent professional—in many instances determines income. But class is about much more than just income level: it also reflects and expresses such parameters as the degree of autonomy exercised in the workplace, the opportunities experienced for intellectual and personal development, the ability to influence the policies or direction of the business, and the quality of the working environment.

In the United States, there is a cadre of blue-collar workers, usually unionized, who enjoy relatively high family incomes. Yet even many of these workers labor under conditions that diminish their ability to play a supportive role at home. Consider the example of a cross-country trucker whose take-home pay may be $60,000 a year or more. For that trucker, relative affluence is bought at the price of long overtime hours, extended periods away from home, few opportunities on the job to develop or explore other talents, and extreme physical fatigue. There are many such working-class jobs in this society that, even when they provide a reasonably good income, leave adults in a very poor position, whether physically, intellectually, or emotionally, to help with their youngsters' academic work.

Unfortunately, the dynamic of class seldom stops even at this point. The parent who cannot help with academic work, or whose life prospects were not enhanced by completion of high school, may bring one of two mind-sets to the request for such help. For some, the demeaning nature of work life may lead to the placing of extreme demands on the child to "make it on your own so that you don't end up like me." The child who is put under such pressure to make it on his or her own, especially when in competition with other children who do not face such an austere burden, may be all the more inclined to rebel against parental or school authority. For other parents, their failure to make it in the work world is proof that school is nothing more than a cruel hoax, a set of arbitrary hurdles to be negotiated simply to gain admission to the rat race. They will often discourage their children from paying close attention to homework, and may resent its intrusions into

family life or even the limits it places on teenage job opportunities, which they see as being more real than the elusive promise of
a rewarding job at some undefined point in the future.

When students respond to such messages either with rebellion
or with apathy, they pose an implicit challenge to the discipline
and rationale of the school. At this point, a range of cultural attitudes regarding work, class, and school comes into play.

From its Puritan beginnings to the present, American society
has celebrated the work ethic. Hard work has been regarded as
either a route to salvation—whether secular or divine—or proof
that one is already saved, because endowed with the right character. Teachers have special reasons to embrace and even intensify
some version of this ethic. Having themselves persevered in a system that imposed continual homework on them, they have a natural, and all too human, tendency to seek to justify their own sacrifices. Charged by the community with preparing students for
the world of work, they want to be able to prove that their standards are strict and that their enforcement of them is strong and
consistent. One consequence of this cultural dynamic is that
homework has become not only an important norm within the
schools, but an accepted indicator of character as well. Judgments
are made as to the inherent worth of a student on the basis of his/
her homework performance. In the process, issues of self-esteem
may arise for the student that go well beyond a specific incident
or failure.

Scholars and researchers have struggled to explain the sky-
high dropout rates in some inner-city and rural communities, the
entrenched disparities in school funding, and the strong correlations between class and academic achievement. Some have suggested that schools may in themselves exacerbate the inequalities
that exist in American society. Many wonder if there are mecha-
nisms in place that serve to make the system less workable for poor
and working-class kids. We believe there are.

PUBLIC SCHOOLS IN A CLASS SOCIETY

The story of how class affects and to a great degree even determines academic achievement and opportunity in our society is a

long and complicated one. In order to understand that story we need to look at the ways in which we structure and govern our schools. We also need to examine some basic beliefs held by Americans. Before we can make meaningful sense of a class analysis of schooling in the United States, we need to think about how we as a society understand class differences.

We suspect that many Americans may be unwilling to acknowledge the existence of an entrenched class system in the United States that serves to constrain or enhance our children's life chances. As a rule, we Americans accept and are fascinated by wealth. We chronicle its sources and accomplishments, but only sporadically do we recognize the ways in which disparities in wealth can work to shape lives. For the most part, Americans have believed that differences in wealth or class position don't matter because our society offers opportunities for tremendous social mobility. If one is very poor today, this thinking holds, it may be just a sometime thing: one has only to work a little harder or get a little more education in order to move up the ladder. Many Americans feel that even if life has some big winners and losers, everyone at least has an even chance to win that great lottery.

Yet detailed studies of economic mobility conducted over the last decade suggest that equality of opportunity in this nation is at best a long shot thing. Some are always more equal than others, even when we're talking about opportunity and not results.

The story of the relationship between class and academic achievement is important to us because homework affects people of different classes differently, and therefore the practice of homework appears to further disadvantage the already disadvantaged.

Americans' belief in class mobility was central to the development of the education system in the Unites States. As early as the nineteenth century, our ideal was a publicly supported education system open to all (except, of course, black slaves and Native Americans). That system would guarantee every child an equal chance of rising to the top of the social pyramid. (Contrast this with schooling in England, where a dual system existed from the beginning, one for laborers and one for the middle and upper classes.) However, many now think of this historical ideal of free and equal American education as part of the "Great School Legend"—in other words, more myth than fact.[3]

In part we cling to the ideal of equal educational opportunity because democracy demands an educated citizenry. In order for a democracy to work, its citizens must be informed participants. In a democratic country with a large immigrant population, education becomes even more crucial, as it is one means of transforming a nation of immigrants into Americans. Because education is about "citizen creating," a strong dose of nationalism is embedded in our curriculum. In fact, much of the resistance we have seen in recent years to bilingual and multicultural education springs from the latent belief that many of us share about the role of education in fostering nationalism.

For all of the above reasons, schooling in the United States is strongly linked to some of our most cherished values, such as democracy and freedom. The vast economic inequities in this country, however, fly in the face of those values. Nevertheless, the ingrained belief in equality leads many Americans to the conviction that if the poor just worked a bit harder, did more homework, and disciplined their social lives a bit better, then they, too, could buy a piece of the American Dream.

We, too, believe that education is about fostering democratic citizenship, but we depart from the conventional norms on a couple of points. Democratic citizenship encompasses both the opportunity and the ability to discuss the merits and limits of the larger political economy, including its modes of work, consumption, and media. It is, in short, more than simply a means of finding work within an economic system whose validity is taken for granted. And it presumes that students have opportunities within the school and life experiences outside it that provide them with the psychological and temporal space to question existing practices. Such an education in democratic citizenship, like political democracy itself, is something for which citizens need perpetually to strive. They cannot assume it as a given or a natural fact of social life in America.

PUBLIC FUNDING AND PUBLIC EDUCATION

My Posse Don't Do Homework

Title of a book by LouAnne Johnson[4]

In her book by this title, the basis for the 1995 movie *Dangerous Minds,* Johnson chronicles her work to motivate and inspire students in an inner-city high school. In this true story, the students move from educational despair to hope, demonstrating that it is possible for poor kids to get on track in school. Over the years, many other educators have documented their own work in poor communities, and theirs are tales of hope and abandonment, joy and despair.[5] The stories told in these books are remarkable precisely because the work of educators in poor communities is so hard. Few of us are familiar with the daily reality in such schools, and while these "against all odds" stories may give us hope, more important is that they serve to remind us of the gross inequities that exist in our country, and of the heroic efforts required to bring effective education to a vast number of American kids.

What equal educational opportunity really means and how it is measured are questions that have plagued for decades. According to James Coleman, the main author of the influential report *Equality of Educational Opportunity,* the very notion of equal educational opportunity has from the beginning been based on a few guiding principles:

1. Education must be free until the point of entry into the job market.
2. Education must provide a common curriculum for all.
3. Students from the same community should attend a common school.
4. Local taxes should support the schools equally within a given locality.[6]

Although most of us probably embrace these ideals, they hardly describe the reality of our educational history. Rather, they are part of the Great School Legend. Let's look at each principle in turn.

Education is never really free for poor kids, as Coleman points out. Families in nineteenth-century America needed the children to work on the farm or, in the case of sons, to apprentice in the father's trade. Coleman found that, curiously, "secondary education interfered with opportunity for working-class children; while it opened up opportunities at higher social levels, it closed them at lower ones."[7] Although this held less true in the twentieth than in the nineteenth century, to this day many working-class kids remain unwilling to forgo the opportunity lost by selecting an academic program over vocational training. Even now, in some rural farm and coastal fishing communities, families need their sons to begin working as soon as they are physically able. Many of these students attend school only sporadically, when their help isn't required on the boats or in the fields.

In this era of tracking and ability groupings starting as early as kindergarten, we may find it hard to believe that there was ever a time when people thought all kids should learn the same things. But that was indeed the case until 1918, when the National Educational Association issued a report entitled *The Seven Cardinal Principles of Education*.[8] In presenting its argument for a revised secondary curriculum, the NEA claimed that if we wanted to educate all of the children in this country, we would have to devise an education more appropriate for the "working classes." This single document managed to move secondary schooling away from the classical education of the nineteenth century toward diversified curriculum that offered different academic programs to different students.

We are all familiar with what has become the "shopping-mall" approach to education, with its many electives and varied tracks. Guidance counselors help students "select" the "appropriate" path through the school program. Many researchers have documented how this process sorts students into tracks based on class, so that poor kids tend to end up in vocational-track programs, and middle- and upper-class kids in college-prep tracks.[9] Coleman points out that the current system is inherently flawed in that it assumes a particular future for a student and then shapes his/her education accordingly.

The challenge to the principle of common schools began in 1896, when the Supreme Court upheld a ruling from the southern states maintaining that separate educational facilities could in fact still be equal. It was not until 1954, in *Brown v. Board of Education of Topeka,* that the Supreme Court reversed itself and asserted that separate school facilities were inherently unequal, a ruling that many believe gave needed strength to the civil rights movement. Coleman suggests that this ruling shifted the way we think about equal educational opportunity: "The Court brought into the open the implicit goals of equality of educational opportunity— that is, goals having to do with the *results* of school—to which the original concept was somewhat awkwardly directed."[10]

According to Coleman, this shift toward results was quickly overshadowed by a push for integration as the sole way to remedy the inequality in schooling in the United States. For a variety of reasons, school integration has been one of America's least successful public policy initiatives. Most Americans still attend schools that are segregated, if not by color, then by class.

The push to end legal segregation, important though it was, did little to address massive class and even racial inequality within American education. It is easy to forget how limited the focus of *Brown* actually was. By ending the practice of legalized segregation, whereby, as in some southern communities, children living in racially mixed neighborhoods were legally mandated to attend separate schools, *Brown* did have an impact on the racial composition of schools. Yet in many northern communities, school segregation had been achieved through residential segregation, and the basic American principle of residential schools effectively replicated the same pattern of school segregation found in the South. By the sixties and seventies, northern liberals were pushing to extend the principles of *Brown* to enable the achievement of greater racial homogeneity in the schools through urban busing programs. Such programs were in themselves not without their problems and unforeseen consequences. Alhough resistance to busing was surely motivated in part by racial animosities, many parents and children simply resented the increased travel time it required, and the loss of focus on neighborhood schools. One result of busing within the urban school districts was a pattern of flight on the part of many middle- and working-class whites to suburban school districts and to newly established private and parochial schools.

The problem of school flight further highlights the context of substantial class inequalities within which issues of school integration have been played out. While *Brown* did leave a legacy of a school system in which there was greater racial balance within many schools, there nonetheless remained vast qualitative differences among those schools. Because our schools are financed so heavily by local property taxes, children whose parents have good jobs and who live in affluent suburban neighborhood settings get to go to far better schools than many of their urban counterparts. These suburban schools may no longer be able to exclude the children of those middle-class blacks who manage to move to the suburbs, but the lack of economic opportunity and the patterns of residential segregation deny such educational opportunities to many minority and working-class children.

Even when children of different class or racial backgrounds do attend the same school, class and race continue to play a major role. Schools that are formally integrated often have elaborate tracking systems that effectively serve to separate out students according to their "ability." Researchers have found, for example, that advanced placement classes and "gifted" programs begin to be introduced and to proliferate at the same time that the schools in these districts were becoming more racially mixed.[11]

Ten years after the *Brown* decision, when our attention had shifted to educational results, educators searched for ways to explain the vast differences in educational achievement between whites and blacks. Mandated by the Civil Rights Act of 1964, the government undertook one of the largest social science research projects in history, headed by Johns Hopkins University sociologist James Coleman. The findings from that study, *Equality of Educational Opportunity,* referred to most often as the Coleman Report, were published in 1966. Recognizing the need to define the terms under study, Coleman's committee split its focus between an analysis of input of resources, facilities, curriculum, and teachers and an analysis of outputs in the form of test scores, reading levels, occupational opportunities. Perhaps the most important and far-reaching conclusion of the Coleman Report was the finding that complete equality of educational opportunity can be reached only if all the divergent out-of-school influences vanish, a condition that would arise only in the environment of boarding schools.[12] The Coleman Report shocked the nation by suggesting that student achievement could not be attributed to school factors alone but was more strongly influenced by factors related to the home environment.[13]

The underlying assumption of much of the work done by the "Great Society" programs spawned by Coleman's committee's research was that poor homes were deficient and the State had a responsibility to "fix" them. This notion laid the groundwork for the compensatory-education programs of the seventies and eighties, which were directed at only the poorest citizens. Based on the belief that deficient home environments could be compensated for by enriched educational environments, such programs granted schools in poor neighborhoods federal funds for everything from free-breakfast initiatives to reading campaigns. In fact, even today researchers use the number of students receiving a free or reduced-rate lunch as an indicator of the socioeconomic status of a community. Funding continues to this day, albeit somewhat scaled back, under the name of Title One, Title Two, and so forth. The longevity of some of these programs gives testifies to our belief that kids from the poorest families deserve a break, and that schools are one place where they should get it.

The rather problematic implications behind the "deficiency" model have been debated for decades. In conceiving it, Coleman no doubt felt he was contributing to the emergence of a more liberal and equitable society, but that legacy is far from secure. Just how simplistic the Great Society approach was is illustrated in the following story: Lady Bird Johnson, as First Lady, paid a visit to an inner-city housing development. Surrounded by a tangle of

TV cameras, Secret Service agents, and assorted politicians, she stopped to ask a little girl her name. The child, blinded by the TV lights and awed by the presence of the First Lady, stood speechless. That evening President Johnson appeared on national television and recounted the event, saying, in effect, that he had found there were blacks in this country who do not know their own name by age six.

The programs of the Great Society are now history. Most of the millions of dollars that went into programs designed to reduce the "deficiency" of the poor no doubt alleviated some real suffering. Some might say, in fact, that the current violence and desperation in our cities are due to the lack of funding for programs that grew out of the findings of Coleman's report.

While we all think that we know what equal educational opportunity means, and we all embrace it, it is really a rather murky concept whose meaning has changed over time. Sometimes confusion over the term itself obscures a rather simple reality of American life: if you are poor, your educational opportunities will be limited. Whether we look at inputs or outputs or tax bases, the message is the same: the poor do not have the same educational opportunities as the rest of us.[14]

YE HAVE THE POOR WITH YOU ALWAYS*
Sociologists speak about the schools' being middle class. Teachers are for the most part middle class and espouse middle-class values. The middle class is comfortable in school, speaks the language of the school, and shares the values embedded in the school day.[15]

Economists have in fact documented the ways in which schools reproduce class relations, especially as they are relate to the workplace. Two such theorists, Samuel Bowles and Herbert Gintis, suggest that

> the major aspects of the structure of schooling can be understood in
> terms of the systemic needs for producing reserve armies of skilled
> labor, legitimating the technocratic-meritocractic perspective, rein-

* Mark 14:7

forcing the fragmentation of groups of workers into stratified status groups, and accustoming youth to the social relationships of dominance and subordinancy in the economic system.[16]

In findings published in 1976, Bowles and Gintis noted that schools in working-class urban neighborhoods were more tightly regimented than their counterparts in suburban neighborhoods. Suburban schools tended to have "greater student participation, less direct supervision . . . and a value system stressing internalized standards of control."[17] Although the authors have been widely criticized for being too rigid in proposing a strict correspondence between education and the economic system, no one really doubts their basic premise: "Schools in the U.S. tailor the self-concepts, aspirations, and social class identifications of individuals to the requirements of the social division of labor."[18]

Research alerts us to the reality of a school system that sorts and divides students not according to their innate ability but rather by their class status, as manifest in the relative wealth of their community, their use of language, their artistic appreciation, and the like. Some researchers have studied the ways in which students operate inside this system, especially how they resist having their future be determined by the school. These "resistance theorists" argue that working-class students create individualized student cultures inside the schools in order to maintain some control over their identity.[19] Typically, however, these students go on to reproduce the cultural attitudes and practices of their own class, often carrying them to an extreme. For example, vocational-track males may elevate manual labor as being inherently "more masculine" than intellectual labor as a way to find comfort in their predetermined destiny.[20]

Tracking is a schooling practice of particular interest to researchers who want to understand how schools reproduce social-class positions. These researchers have uncovered the class bias in various teaching techniques used in different high school tracks. In the higher-track classes, for instance, students are asked more open-ended questions and given more freedom to explore topics than their counterparts in lower-level tracks. Reportedly, school personnel rationalize this by saying that the lower-track kids will need to learn to follow orders and the upper-track kids will need to learn to give them.[21]

Educators justify the use of tracking by arguing that track placement is based on ability. We would be inclined to respond that ability is multifaceted and cannot be measured along one dimension. Certain abilities can also be nurtured or suppressed by a student's home and vocational experiences. Our schools often recognize and emphasize only a rather narrow range of skills that meet the current needs and preferences of the social elite. Moreover, they neglect the role that a student's environment may have played in the unequal development of even the preferred set of skills.

HOMEWORK AND TRACKING

Privileged parents who hold the levers of power on school boards and committees see increased homework as a means for their children to raise their level of academic achievement and perhaps better their chances of getting ahead in the college admission competition.

This state of affairs may go some way toward explaining why there has been no organized revolt over homework. Privileged parents have the resources to hire tutors and provide other kinds of assistance that will enable their children to complete their homework. For their part, working-class and poor parents are effectively silenced by the public school system.[22] Because they are not professionals, their concerns are often discounted by school officials and teachers. And since the working class has historically been less politically powerful in America than the middle and upper classes, its collective voice is often not heard in political arenas. Taken together, all these factors compel many parents to seek individual solutions: we all hope that if we manage our time better, get sick less, and maybe move into a bigger house, we can help our kids do their homework. With homework appearing on the national agenda only in the guise of the call for higher academic standards, questioning its value becomes even harder.

Like tracking, homework is a practice that perpetuates the

social-class inequity that seems to be built into schooling. When we look at homework in the context of a poor student's life, the practice seems almost abusive. Dropouts in Etta's study talked about the life stresses on the rural poor. They spoke of having to cook dinner for their families, having to watch younger children, having to care for sick parents. In their world, homework simply didn't fit in. They could make it to school each day—that is, provided their cars kept working—but doing schoolwork after hours just wasn't possible.

Homework further disadvantages these children by assuming that they have a "quiet, well-lit place" in which to study. If we all need a quiet, well-lit place to study, far away from the TV, we would like to suggest that we know a perfect spot that precisely meets those requirements: the schoolhouse.

The amount of ink spilled to date on the subject of how to get one's kids to do their homework indicates that it must be a difficult task for everyone, not just the working class and the poor. We must acknowledge that students return home to very different environments with vastly different resources. Homework takes time, space, study aids, and very particular academic skills, resources that are by no means equally distributed across American communities.[23]

Homework in the Global Economy

> My view of the world, our country, and our country's needs is dia-
> metrically opposite of yours. I cannot imagine a shorter work week.
> I can imagine a longer one both in school and at work if America is
> to be competitive in the first half of the next century.
>
> A Fortune 500 CEO, quoted in Juliet Schor,
> *The Overworked American*[1]

Although homework causes much anguish in many homes, not
only for children but also for their parents, it is one of our most
entrenched institutional practices. Despite periodic attempts to
lighten the load or redistribute the burden, few efforts to reform
homework have met with any real success.

Homework persists despite the lack of any solid evidence that
it achieves its much-touted gains, and even amid much confusion
as to just what those gains should be. When a social practice becomes a virtual icon of the culture, it is likely that something beyond a specific policy debate or practical need is at stake. The value
that our culture attaches to homework must therefore lie in more
than just its purported ability to make our children more capable
students.

Homework is part of a larger narrative about the changing nature of the U.S. economy and America's place in the world. The
policy aims of U.S. business and political leaders have been sustained by that narrative for most of the last two decades. These
aims have met increasing resistance as their implications for Americans' quality of life have become more evident. Nonetheless,
without a more fully elaborated alternative narrative, such resis-

tance is likely to be sporadic at best, and written off as little more than a parochial and ill-informed reaction to modernity and globalization. It will leave no lasting mark.

If reductions in and reforms of homework are not accompanied in relatively short order by other economic reforms, young workers will continue limping along in the corporate global economy. Parents will still have too little time to pursue any cultural, educational, or recreational agendas with their children. In such a context, business leaders and educational traditionals could successfully renew their calls for intensified homework as the only way for our young people to escape their difficult circumstances.

Because school and homework play so pivotal a role in current elite narratives, basic alterations to either are unlikely unless and until these struggles can be situated in alternative understandings of the global economy, the centrality of material growth, and the importance of work itself to social and individual identity. We do not claim finality for our counternarratives, and we suspect that no narrative vision could or should ever be final or all-embracing. Nonetheless, we do assert that a politics in which such questions as these are laid on the table for democratic debate must be a healthier one.

GLOBAL DREAMS AND NIGHTMARES

Pundits and politicians regularly celebrate the "globalization" of our economy, telling a tale of new products and prosperity. Nor is their faith in this new global economy confined to economics narrowly conceived. Going as far back as Montesquieu in the eighteenth century, global trade has been viewed as the ultimate route to peace. Former Harvard economics professor and current Under Secretary of the Treasury Lawrence Summers recently endorsed this perspective on trade with the following remark: "I think you will find that successful economic growth and economic integration is [*sic*] the best way mankind has yet found to produce stability."[2]

So far, however, this new global economy has been most successful in bringing Third World inequalities home to the United States. The most recent studies in this area indicate that while the top 10 percent of our society has enjoyed enormous increases in wealth, the remaining 90 percent has seen no such gain, and the bottom 20 percent has actually *lost* economic ground. The process of global economic integration under way today is a sure route to even greater economic inequality, not only in the advanced Western nations but also in the so-called Third World societies. Eventually this growing economic inequality will pose a threat to democracy itself, as will the rise of various forms of destructive nationalism and racism, which this new international regime paradoxically fosters.

Expanded trade *could* promote needed economic development, a more stable world, and a better quality of life for all, but these gains would be possible only through democratic reforms of our corporate trade practices and corporate workplaces. School reform and a better understanding of the role that schools play in fostering democratic citizenship are integral to that process.

Paradoxically, good jobs and good quality of life may require that schools look beyond their obsessive preoccupation with making each of our children more hardworking and more skilled in order to participate more effectively in the global marketplace. That marketplace itself, with its values and demands, may need to be curbed and reshaped, and if so, it may be only those citizens whose cultural and personal lives have embraced a wider range of circumstances and aspirations who will be willing and able to undertake the task.

The loss of many formerly well-paid factory jobs and the stagnation or decline in working-class income have had social and educational consequences as well. The economic gap between declining inner cities and affluent suburbs has grown and antagonisms have intensified. Many suburban communities now literally wall themselves off from their poorer neighbors. Even the most modest commitment to equal-educational funding is met with arguments laden with hostility toward poor and minority communities. Lacking even the most minimal contact with poorer citizens, more affluent Americans find it easier and easier to demonize them.

In a society in which educational opportunity depends on

public schools, and in which those schools are financed primarily by local property taxes, great economic inequality translates into limited educational opportunities. Where jobs are scarce, property values are low and schools are underfunded. Since housing in this country has traditionally been segregated not only by racial or ethnic identity but by income as well, declines in working-class incomes have differential effects on particular communities.

The "savage inequalities" that author Jonathan Kozol describes are rooted in the uneven development of our economy— so that, for example, regions dependent upon traditional manufacturing employment have suffered immensely in recent years.[3] Such growing inequalities, combined with the tendency to seek private escapes from social problems, may diminish the will to finance public education at all. As better-off parents either leave declining urban areas or send their children to private schools, the likelihood decreases that those schools will continue to receive full funding. And as the schools become more disadvantaged, the cycle begins again, as negative views of public education are once more confirmed.

Experts in both industrial organization and community development have argued that downgrading jobs, increasing inequalities within the workplace and thus among communities, seeking low-wage havens abroad, and stretching hours are not the only ways to compete in the new global economy. They have touted an alternative model, the "high-performance workplace," which differs in several important aspects from conventional business organizations. Advocates of high-performance workplaces have identified a cluster of related characteristics as being essential to their success. These include the use of flexible technologies; some form of worker participation or teamwork; ongoing worker education and training; a commitment to employment security and good working conditions; a narrowing of the gap in both income and responsibilities between workers and managers; quality consciousness; and active role for unions and employee committees in achieving gains in the production process. Workers themselves help design personnel policies and fashion flexible, family-friendly work schedules. Contrary to the expectations of many traditional business leaders, such enterprises have consistently proved more efficient in the long run.

Unfortunately, such workplaces have been the exception rather than the rule in the U.S. economy, though they are quite prevalent in some social democratic cultures, notably Sweden. They are unusual in the United States for at least two reasons. Although the firms themselves are more productive and efficient, they do require more sharing of power and profits; historically, they have tended to proliferate only where democratic unions have real power and governments place an effective floor under workers' economic rights.

Equally fundamentally, the creation of high-performance workplaces entails major start-up costs and a commitment to the long term. With U.S. corporate management now heavily affected by short-term changes in stock prices, which are driven in turn by the role of mutual funds and even international capital flows in our markets, too few managers can take the long-term view.

The rote and restrictive nature of work life within many corporate enterprises, not only for blue-collar but for many white-collar and service-sector jobs as well, is a primary reason that reliance on educational reforms as an exclusve strategy for economic change is misplaced. If the current direction of the U.S. economy remains unchanged, the vast majority of U.S. students, no matter how they acquire basic skills and broader analytic reasoning in school, will have too few opportunities to deploy them in the course of their daily working lives.

If current business practices and priorities prevail, many workers and communities will continue to lag behind. School boards and parents eager to pursue homework reform will then find themselves in a difficult bind. Even the best academic research on the limits of homework may not sway the current generation of business leaders, who are deeply committed to long-hour jobs and want a work force that is psychologically prepared for and fully accepting of those requirements. Unfortunately, more homework may then seem the best, and least expensive, way to please business leaders and thus help ready working- and middle-class children for the few secure and challenging jobs that remain.

THE CORPORATE WORKPLACE, HOMEWORK, AND CONSUMERISM

Along with Harvard economist Juliet Schor, we would argue that free markets underproduce leisure time. And as the distinguished labor historian Stanley Aronowitz has pointed out, the shrinkage of leisure time within corporate workplaces was a major concern of early and radically democratic factions within the American labor movement. Schor's analysis of market capitalism and Aronowitz's examination of labor history have important implications for the homework debate. One consequence of an economy with substantial unemployment is that employers have the power not only to cut and downgrade jobs but also to lengthen the hours of the jobs that are left. The two strategies go hand in hand. Jobs with long hours serve the interests of employers because they minimize training costs, and job cuts create a pool of unemployed workers desperate for work. Knowing that others are willing to step in makes it harder, in turn, for the employed to protest the conditions of their employment.

Schor's recent work *The Overspent American* identifies some further factors that lead to the intensification of the work-and-spend cycle, to pressures on adults and children to work long hours, and to the desertion of the public sector as an appropriate vehicle for resolution of these problems.[4]

Schor's fundamental premise is that as social beings, we are lost without some set of socially constructed norms to guide us. In a society in which some version of the Protestant work ethic has always valorized work and the material success that is its just reward, getting and spending have added meaning to life. More to the point, they have also often been an expression of individuality, another distinctly American phenomenon.

Keeping up with the Joneses is more American than apple pie. In the fifties and sixties, it may have occasioned the kind of bland

and sometimes oppressive conformity symbolized by Levittown, but the standards were often set as much by neighbors as by any distant authority. And in neighborhoods where income differentials were relatively small, the standards could be met by many.

Today's consumerism is qualitatively far more problematic, and the role of the neighborhood in our lives is much less substantial. Even in two-parent families, Mom is ever less likely to be at home. Mom and Dad are both working, and the Joneses with whom they hope to keep up are coworkers and supervisors. For almost everyone, television with its ads and opulent life styles is the new neighborhood.

We would argue that the current stress on homework and the long school day may be another, and increasingly problematic, form of the preparation demanded by our corporate and consumer society—a way to accustom the student worker to long working hours. Not only is homework itself a form of psychological preparation, but both its form and its content seem designed to send the cardinal message of today's business civilization: *This is a competitive world whose purpose lies in endless production.* Our ability to multiply material affluence is portrayed as proof of our ability to know and control that world, and thus testifies to our personal rectitude.

The form and content of the message distract us from the fact that human decisions and cultural values have made that competitive world what it is, and that social choices have turned economic growth into an imperative that shapes our lives. Far less successful is the attempt to still the doubts and resentments that many of us harbor regarding what we must give up in order to sustain this business civilization.

CHAPTER 7

What's a Mother— and a Neighborhood, and a Nation—to Do?

There are ways out of the economic, psychological, and philo-sophical trap posed by the burgeoning demands of schools, work-places, and corporate global agendas. More homework won't nec-essarily make children better students, and even if it did, they wouldn't be assured of getting better or more remunerative jobs when they reached adulthood. Longer working hours for their parents will not resolve the insecurity and injustice inflicted by modern corporations and unregulated global markets. The inten-sification of homework and school is both a rationalization of and a preparation for a corporate world in need of fundamental re-form. With that in mind, what course should we follow around the kitchen table, in our neighborhoods, and in our broader pol-itics?

We ought to start with a lesson learned from the New Deal. Market economies work best when they provide a reasonable safety net for all citizens, so that genuine economic opportu-nity and minimal levels of consumer power, on which stability is premised, are preserved. If we are really concerned about what our children learn, we must devote far more attention to the con-ditions under which they do that learning. There is no more seri-ous barrier to learning than poverty.

Rates of childhood poverty in this country have reached stag-gering highs. The macro-level inequalities we have discussed in this book have their most severe impact on the lives of children.[1]

If we genuinely want American children to prosper in a global economy, we must provide a minimal level of security for their parents, and we must give families the opportunity to spend some time together. To those ends, we must place some limits on the demands now being made by schools, corporations, and global markets. Since all of these are human creations, we believe it must be possible to redesign them better to meet our needs.

One approach that merits study here is Juliet Schor's recent thinking on how to curb the psychic pressures and practical demands that modern consumer society imposes on many workers. Schor recommends actions along three lines. On an individual level, we can think carefully before making purchases, taking time to scrutinize manufacturer claims and to reflect on what our motives are and whether we wish to or must endorse such motives. On a neighborhood level, Schor suggests that when we need certain types of products, such as riding lawnmowers (now found in nearly every garage in many suburban communities), we might consider whether they could be owned in common by a small group of neighborhoods. (The lending library, which now often offers tapes and CDs among its circulating items, could serve as a model for such common ownership.) Finally, on a national level, Schor advocates the establishment of policies that would reduce our need to purchase particular kinds of goods or address the adverse social and ecological consequences of those purchases. Now, what if we applied these same recommendations to homework?

WHAT'RE A MOTHER AND HER NEIGHBORS TO DO?

> Are you listening to "experts" instead of trusting your instincts and your heart?
>
> Anne Cassidy, author of *Parents Who Think Too Much*[2]

The public's reliance on experts in the second half of the twentieth century has been well documented by social scientists. In education this trend was reflected in the shift away from parents and toward schools as the primary socializing and educating entity.[3] Experts have a role in all social areas, to be sure; a world lacking the benefits of some specialization and detailed study would clearly be less productive and less efficient. But even the most detached and scholarly of experts brings to his/her field of study a particular set of interests and values. In turn, we as citizens and parents have both a right and an obligation to make known our own values and concerns and, whenever possible, to shape the parameters that will govern future study and recommendations.

In her book *Parents Who Think Too Much*, Anne Cassidy gives hope to parents who have been caught in the "expert" trap. Citing the rise in conferences, classes, seminars, and workshops for parents, Cassidy implores her readers to treat all such advice with skepticism. Above all else, she suggests that we spend enough time with our children to really get to know them; it is through this knowledge, she promises, that we will grow as parents. To this end she recommends that we cut back on work, limit our children's activities, or even move to the country—anything that will give us more downtime with our kids. She avoids big prescriptions, which would go against her basic belief in parenting by instinct, but her underlying concerns should strike a chord with all parents who want to reclaim their lives, and their children's, from the impositions of work, school, and the media.

Homework seems to us a key piece in that puzzle. By clearing the kitchen table, parents can make a space in which to create a family, to define themselves, and to chart a course for their children. The time this would free up for families would allow parents to construct a life of their own choosing for themselves and their children.

How do we begin to work our way out of the labyrinth of issues that surround homework? How do we put the issue of homework on the national political agenda and get politicians to move beyond mouthing the rhetoric of "family values" to actually doing something for families? How do we raise the issue of homework at our schools without being seen as meddling parents?

Perhaps our first step should be to talk to our friends. We are convinced that for many parents, homework is a classic instance of what C. Wright Mills referred to as a seemingly private trouble that is in fact widely shared and is thus in need of becoming a public issue.[4] Parents might discuss among themselves some of the questions we have posed for future survey research. These include 1) how much time their children spend on homework; 2) what the nature of that homework is, and what they see it as contributing to the child's intellectual development; 3) what opportunities are lost to homework—that is, what other activities or experiences, including recreation, conversations with parents or parents' friends, social life, jobs, volunteer commitments, and so on must be forgone in order to meet homework demands; 4) what impact homework has on the child's health, rest, and sense of well-being, 5) what impact it has on the friendliness and civility of family life.

In many respects, the women's movement of the sixties may be instructive here. As Mills's essay "The Darling Little Slave"[5] famously suggested, many women once experienced their lives as lonely and lacking in stimulation or purpose. Not only were many middle-class wives limited entirely to a domestic role, but the importance of that role itself inexorably shrank in a world of schools, extracurricular activities, packaged foods, and commercial clothing. A great number of these women regarded themselves as psychologically troubled or personally unfit. But in the context of sixties politics, many came to recognize that they shared a similar discontent, and that realization changed both the nature of their unhappiness and the form of response they themselves deemed appropriate.

The same process might enable parents to overcome the shame and guilt that the school system often causes them to feel. Many of us have been told by school personnel that if we just had homework rules in place, everything would be fine. Homework problems are routinely reported as our failure. Books, magazine articles, and handouts from school all try to place pressure on families to establish routines for homework that will, they assure us, end the homework wars. Most of us know better. When we share our experiences with others, we come to see that the fault is not ours but that of a system that sets up expectations that we cannot possibly meet. Overcoming shame will allow us to take the next step: organizing action-oriented discussion groups.

Parents may want to start by establishing informal discussion groups. The existing structure of the PTA could provide a forum for a community-wide discussion of problems related to homework. Each community has a particular set of issues that is in some way unique to it. In rural areas, for example, the homework problem is exacerbated by long bus commutes. In some places, the pressure to excel drives homework overload, while in others the rhetoric is based on "catching up." Through informal discussion groups, community members can identify the issues they wish to bring before the school board or to raise with school personnel. Communities also need to identify resources that can be strengthened so students will have activities available to them after school.

Based on the many conversations we have had with parents and students and our own experiences, we believe that several reasonable guidelines can be laid down for homework. We are absolutely convinced that homework is almost always counterproductive for elementary school children and should not be given to them. The standard school day itself is long enough for these youngsters and often leaves them exhausted. By the time they get to middle school, an 8:00-to-2:00 day might be supplemented by an hour of personal academic work in school, along lines we will elaborate below.

For high school students, our first and foremost principle is that school-related activities should never take up more than forty hours a week. This includes such activities as required physical-education classes as well as more typical academic work. We recognize that if students are on sports teams, they may have "away" games that keep them doing school-related work from six-thirty in the morning until eight or nine at night. But we count that as the student's choice and therefore as part of his or her leisure time.

As early as 1938, this nation determined that more than forty hours' work a week posed a threat to an adult's health and productivity. Why shouldn't the same logic apply to the high school student? We believe that much of what is gained by older kids through homework could equally be achieved within the framework of a forty-hour school week. If classes ran from eight until two, the student could receive help in school on designated projects from two until four. Since teachers themselves are often over-worked, assistance of this sort could be provided by hiring extra staff and/or drawing on other members of the community with special gifts in the subject area. Teachers could have a more flexible work schedule, and some might choose to work with individual students on guided study.

After-school programs need to be put in the context of two other vital educational issues: equal school funding and school choice. We are opposed to current voucher proposals, which would virtually privatize our schools and disproportionately benefit the rich. Nonetheless, there is a clear argument to be made for fostering greater opportunities for choice within public school systems, perhaps along the lines sketched out by educator Deborah Meier.[6] Particular schools within a local school district could adopt not only different curriculum policies and emphases but also different policies regarding homework. Those parents and children who were most interested in such an initiative would thus have a chance to participate in it without forcing doubters to join them.

Unfortunately, no reform of homework, especially one emphasizing more individual help within the school, is going to work for schools that are already badly overcrowded and under-staffed. School-board level mobilization around homework issues will also have to involve politics at the state level to assure more adequate and equal funding of schools. We believe, and shall argue below, that such inadequacies require a federal effort as well.

To the extent that we succeed in lengthening the school day slightly and limiting homework, the work of the school will be confined to the schoolhouse and the problems outlined in this book will begin to diminish. We recognize the difficulties associated with changing the school schedule. The loudest protests will come from those who teach "extracurricular" activities such as drama, music, and sports. Many will complain that students need the break from school activities that such programs provide. With some creative planning, however, it should be possible to accommodate the needs of the community.

We can expect Congress to call for a longer school day sometime soon. The proposal will no doubt be driven by the rhetoric of higher standards. Parents should support such efforts only to the extent that they offer relief from homework.

In our political system, such changes will have to be achieved not merely at the state level but school board by school board. Although this may seem a slow process, we would do well to remember that state and local politics still retains the possibility of becoming an experiment in democracy. As homework reforms and other, similar policies improve the quality of life in particular communities, they are bound to spread. And if our arguments are wrong, and the changes we propose do not enhance lives? Well, experimenting in a few communities will hardly be catastrophic.

Parents need to sit in on school board meetings and bring their concerns to the attention of the board. Board meetings are open to the public, and the views of interested citizens are solicited. Some will charge that citizens are too apathetic to attend such meetings, but we disagree. Even in an era when voter participation in congressional and gubernatorial elections is at an all-time low, local school board races and actions often elicit great parent interest. Whether it be a contentious social issue such as school prayer or the elimination of sex education, or a more mundane topic such as new construction or school budget, citizens will turn out. As parents turn up at meetings, relate their concerns about homework, and manage to free up some time to impart their own views to their children, some of the ugliness and divisiveness surrounding those other social issues may even abate. Furthermore, the very ability to win, at the local level, some unstructured time may well convince citizens that political activity can produce rewards, even as it provides more opportunity for such activity.

The process of fostering change on this issue is one in which we must strive for allies. Although it is clear that a majority of teachers still support conventional notions that more is better with regard to homework, we have found a significant minority of doubters. Teachers have an immense stake in this debate, but a surprising number of them report that they believe the push for homework *comes from the parents*. Parents should talk to the teachers in their children's schools and identify those who are willing to listen.

Alliances between teachers and parents can be a powerful force at school board meetings. Teachers' resources, too, are often stretched thin, and their own opportunities to develop and extend their knowledge of a subject or their teaching methods may be lost to long hours spent grading virtually identical papers. We hope that this book will be read by teachers, and that they will be receptive to the more extensive and detailed survey research we are proposing—studies on who does homework, what effects it has on children and families, and what implications it carries for long-term emotional and personal development.

Finally, of course, no political action can produce immediate results. Here as in many other situations, a parent may just have to do whatever he or she can for the benefit of his/her child. "Just say no" may rightly apply as much to homework as to dangerous drugs. One of us has a friend who often sends her daughter to school with a note saying that she didn't do her homework because she was too busy or too tired or had family obligations. We know another parent who has more than once done math homework herself to save her crying or desperate child from censure at school. Parents can reclaim their family space by small measures.

Even at the level of street blocks and neighborhoods, parents can take some constructive steps even before school boards act. Just as neighborhoods can pool resources such as lawnmowers or books, so too can parents form collectives for "consciousness raising" regarding homework.

THE FAMILY AND AMERICAN POLITICS

However important individual, or neighborhood, or even school board strategies are, we believe that their success will be sustainable only if they are accompanied by other, broader political reforms. Even if local school boards take all the steps we recommend, not all children will prosper in this global economy. In a political economy that has always worshiped unregulated markets and individual initiative, poverty and insecurity evoke one constant response: *Your life will be better if you'll just try harder.* Thus we must use the discussion of the quality of life around the kitchen table to broaden our focus and to look at the current rules of corporate capitalism and the global economy. We believe children will be unable to thrive in that economy unless they and their parents have adequate safety nets in the form of job security, assistance for child and elder care, more democratic workplaces, and fairer rules of international trade.

Despite the conservative tenor of the last two decades, one progressive initiative is now making a comeback: proposals to expand the coverage or the amount of the minimum wage are on the table not only in Washington but in many state capitals. An adequate minimum wage is the single most important and most immediately achievable step that can be taken at both state and national levels to address the poverty of families and thus ensure conditions in which young students are more likely to thrive.

The current politics of child care and Social Security are another arena in which appropriate federal policy can improve the quality of life for all families. Rather than blaming "deficiencies" in particular families for their children's educational failure, politicians must recognize that most families today operate under constraints that make the rearing and education of children extremely difficult. As baby boomers age, more working Americans will struggle with the twin burdens of a young family and aging parents. Conservatives maintain that government can no longer afford to be generous to both; they detect a sort of generational triage whereby the needs of kids are not being met because older Americans are laughing all the way to the bank with their exorbitant Social Security checks.

We draw different conclusions. The poverty rate among older Americans is lower than among other segments of the population, but that is precisely because Social Security has played a role in mitigating the worst inequalities and vicissitudes of a market society. We should not and cannot resolve the very real problems of the young by weakening a safety net that has served its purpose. Our wealthy society has the resources to meet the basic needs of our children *and* of our elderly; what is lacking is the political will to fund those needs through equitable taxation.

Social Security is a model for the kind of support that should be provided to our citizens in childhood as well as in old age. By following that model, we can build the political will to sustain equitable taxation and adequate funding for future child-care initiatives. When children's needs have been met, support for the elderly may be more easily defended.

A child-care initiative responsive to the Social Security model would strive for greater universality. It would provide a credit to parents of all preschool-age children and a flat grant to those whose incomes were too low to be taxed. This allowance should be at least several times higher than the current $500 tax credit. A program modeled on these lines would cost more, to be sure, but its universality would ease some of the tensions between at-home parents and those in the conventional labor market. Given a reasonably generous credit, parents would have more flexibility to choose among stay-at-home care, small cooperatives made up of parents who worked part time, or day care in a larger setting.

Ultimately, of course, resolving the child-care crisis requires that we redress one of its major causes: the number of hours most parents have to work. Even the best-run schools or day-care facilities aren't likely to serve children as well without periodic parental involvement, and that means more time must be freed up for parents. Eliminating mandatory overtime, requiring employers to offer reductions in hours as a possible alternative to increased wages, and doubling compensation time for overtime are a few possible correctives for long work hours. These strategies would also serve to create more jobs for those who are currently unemployed or underemployed.

On another level, we also question whether the overlong working day of the student is the best way to develop the kind of creative work force that will prevail in the global economy. No one is denying that basic skills are important, but advances in any field depend on more than mere skill acquisition. Creative individuals often spend a substantial part of their lives on free-ranging reflection, recreation, and a range of cultural activities not related to their main field of endeavor.

We suspect that tying children to long homework regimes has a purpose other than that stated by most of homework's defenders. On some level it seems intended to accustom them, early on, to the long working days that characterize our current political economy. Those (perhaps a large majority) who cannot even as children successfully carry out their perpetual tasks can then be held up as examples, with their very failures cited to rationalize and justify their continuing marginal status within the U.S. economy. Within such a framework, debate must fixate either on how more adequately to monitor and encourage homework (the liberal remedy) or on the permanent—perhaps even genetic or racial—inadequacy of those who most often fail (the conservative answer). In either case, children and their parents are being blamed for problems whose origins in fact lie within corporate workplaces and the demands of the new global economy.

We as reformers would ask parents a further question: Are you really happy in careers that consume most of your lives outside the home and in regimens within the home that control much of your interaction with your children? If the answer is no, isn't there some rationale for striving both individually and as part of a larger movement to limit both work and homework? We believe that at least some parents are becoming more receptive to these questions, and we propose that to the extent that more relaxation could be achieved around the kitchen table, citizens would feel less of a need to support narrow and punitive forms of discipline for workers and other community members who do not meet their every expectation and standard.

Finally, these considerations suggest some of the reasons for our conviction that homework issues cannot be neatly separated from such seemingly unrelated themes as workplaces and the global economy. From the President to powerful corporate executives, everyone is saying that our kids must get a better education and study harder if they are to prevail in the global marketplace. Even if we could win, for a time, the debate as to whether "studying harder" at home really does improve academic and job performance, the continuing stagnation of the global economy and the declining fortunes of workers within it will lead to continual political pressure to blame some aspect of working-class life, unless and until there is a broader reform of corporations and that global economy. As long as our corporate economy remains unjust and undemocratic, those pressures will find a way of persisting around the kitchen table. Failing progress in other areas, we fear that the pressure to impose more work on our children will continue to grow within our educational and political systems. Ultimately, educational practices and systems must accord with our economic order; if that economic order does not become more just and humane, public education will be little more than a handmaiden of narrow corporate imperatives.

PROSPECTS FOR CHANGE

It is our hope that the arguments presented in this book will lead some parents and educators to consider the possibility that homework has been overrated as a schooling intervention. Research does not support the increasing emphasis on homework, and in fact, some studies suggest that it may even be counterproductive at the elementary level. When homework is examined in the context in which it actually occurs, it begins to take on a very different look. Much of the mindless work of homework is simply not useful. More complex homework, in contrast, often demands supervision by trained educators—not by parents, who may be limited in their ability to help their children complete the assignments.

Teachers, often overburdened themselves, may assign as homework whatever is left unfinished at the end of the school day. Homework of this sort transfers the responsibility of education from the school to the family. In this regard, helping with homework is a form of unpaid labor for parents, who have their own educational agendas that reach far beyond the state-mandated curriculum.

We have of course heard the familiar refrain that without lengthy homework, children will simply spend more time in front of the television. Much the same argument has been advanced with regard to shortening the working hours of adults. Certainly, increased TV time will be a possibility for some, but in our eyes, the amount of television watched has many causes.

One factor is fatigue itself. How many even very well educated and serious adults simply "veg out" in front of the TV when they are tired? For children, deciding whether to watch TV or engage in other pursuits will often depend on the available alternatives. When children are well rested, when there is a range of cultural or recreational activities on offer and other kids with whom to play, sing, or do art projects, kids will—and do—gravitate to such activities. But our work-and-spend culture is surely one of the greatest limits to such opportunities. Breaking that work-and-spend cycle and creating opportunities that are more varied and rewarding than television are tasks for broader political intervention and activism. Breaking the hold of homework, however, would allow for a more immediate, and perhaps a more richly rewarding, personal freedom for both parents and children.

Perhaps the greatest drawback of homework for many parents is the strain it places on family life. We all know that when a child is struggling to complete homework, the tension that results can affect all members of the family and even cause lasting breaks in familial relations. Parents have been led to believe that homework is a sign of good teaching, or that when their children spend long hours hitting the books at home, they are "being prepared for the real world." Consequently, we as parents may be caught in a state of cognitive dissonance, asking for something that is fundamentally at odds with our own interests.

History teaches us that homework has not always been seen as a panacea for improving education. Attention to the needs of the whole child has often led educators to stress that other life experiences are central to the healthy development of the child, though today, increasingly, such experiences must be forgone in order to complete the work of the school. Many of us would love to hear from our pediatricians that schoolwork is causing our children's ill health, and had we lived in 1919 instead of 1999, we might have been told just that.

The class divides that plague our country are widened and deepened by the practice of homework. Children who lack academic resources at home are at a distinct disadvantage when schoolwork comes home. In this regard, school practices serve to further intensify the already massive class division. Rather than foster equality, schools unwittingly heighten inequality. Americans who profess a belief in equality of educational opportunity must acknowledge that in order to have the greatest opportunity, students must have equal access to academic resources for the completion of schoolwork.

Genuine education is about more than producing skilled workers; it is about democratic citizenship. Democratic citizenship, for its part, goes far beyond curricular development. Education for democratic citizenship involves preparing citizens to participate in active debate on urgent matters both as students and as young adults. Such participation is less likely when students have spent too many of their waking hours dominated by the demands of school, and too few trying to forge a stronger sense of their social selves, with all the possibilities and limits those selves contain.

Let's return to the stories that began this book. Remember Beth, the parent who was told that schoolwork must take priority over all other activities for her child? Imagine how happy Beth would be to have her daughter's fifth-grade teacher suggest that she do her writing journal on the work she's doing in Hebrew class, and ask that she share with her classmates the new Hebrew words she learns each week.

Remember Bob, Greg's dad, whose once close relationship with his son has eroded because he never sees him? If Greg had his evenings free, he and his dad could share a bowl of popcorn as they watched a baseball game on TV. Bob could tell him his favorite World Series story and recount the history of Fenway Park and the legend of the trading of Babe Ruth. They could agree to get tickets to the next game in their town, and discover they share a love of baseball nurtured by earlier years of playing catch together in the front yard.

Imagine what would happen if all the doctors who have been

treating all kids for back and neck pain banded together and issued a health warning about heavy backpacks. Maybe the organization Physicians for Social Responsibility will replace the *Ladies' Home Journal* as the platform for a new health-based antihomework crusade.

Remember Daniel, who wanted to be on the search-and-rescue team? What if instead of fretting over his homework, Daniel spent an afternoon and evening helping to rescue a young boy lost in the park? Who can tell what the long-term impact might be of saving someone's life?

And what if Margie did all of her math problems in the classroom, where her teacher could see she was struggling and needed a teacher's help to learn fractions? Neither Margie nor her friend Edna would need to resort to cheating, and Margie would actually learn to do the problems rather than "get away" with cribbing the answers.

As we were working on this book, Etta was interviewed on public radio. She commented that baking cookies at night with her son might just be more important than fighting with him over his unfinished math homework. A number of people who heard the broadcast were horrified that an educator could think that baking cookies was more important than doing homework. But in the end, we believe that the quality of our relationships with our children is enhanced by those moments of participating in the activities of daily life. They are the transforming times in our relationships with our children, and without them, we lose touch with each other. We inhabit the same space without knowing one another.

NOTES

Preface

1. "A Real Pain in the Neck: Kids with Heavy Backpacks Should Lighten Up!" *Time for Kids,* October 29, 1999, 7.

Introduction

1. Maria L. La Ganga, "Kicking Homework Out of School: Half Moon Bay Considers Abolishing an Educational Icon," *Los Angeles Times*, October 27, 1994, Home Section, part A.

2. Barry Bluestone and Stephen Rose, "Overworked and Underemployed: Unraveling an Economic Enigma," *The American Prospect* 31 (March–April 1997): 58–69.

3. Jonathan Kozol, *Savage Inequalities: Children in America's Schools* (New York: Crown, 1991).

1. The Kitchen Table

1. R. A. Paschal, T. Weinstein, and H. J. Walberg, "The Effects of Homework on Learning: A Quantitative Synthesis," *The Journal of Educational Research* 78, no. 2 (November–December 1994): 97.

2. Sharon Begley, "Homework Doesn't Help," *Newsweek*, March 30, 1998, 50.

3. R. P. McDermott, S. V. Goldman, and H. Varanne, "When School Goes Home: Some Problems in the Organization of Homework," *Teachers College Record* 85, no. 3 (spring 1984): 396.

4. John Taylor Gatto, *Dumbing Us Down: The Hidden Curriculum of Compulsory Schooling* (Philadelphia: New Society Publishers, 1992), 74.

5. "Playing Their Parts: Parents and Teachers Talk about Parental Involvement in Public Schools." (http://www.publicagenda.org/aboutpa3t.html)

6. David Davenport, "Let Children Be Children, Not Bookworms: Kids Are Right about Homework," *The Cincinnati Enquirer*, August 23, 1998.

7. David Davenport, "More Homework Won't Help," *Bangor Daily News,* August 7, 1998, A11.

8. "Family Student and Assignment Characteristics of Positive Homework Experiences," paper presented at annual meeting of the American Educational Research Association, San Diego, Calif., April 1998, 16.

9. Jianzhong Xu, "Doing Homework: A Study of Possibilities," master's thesis, Columbia University Teachers College, 1994.

10. Lyn Corno, "Homework Is a Complicated Thing," *Educational Researcher* 25, no. 8 (November 1996): 28.

11. F. M. Levine and K. M. Anesko, *Winning the Homework War* (Englewood Cliffs, N.J.: Prentice-Hall, 1987).

12. C. Wright Mills, *The Sociological Imagination* (New York: Oxford University Press, 1959).

13. W. K. Hoy and A. E. Woolfolk, "Teachers' Sense of Efficacy and the Organizational Health of Schools," *The Elementary School Journal* 93, no. 4 (March 1993): 355−372; J. G. M. Imants and C. J. DeBrabander, "Teachers' and Principals' Sense of Efficacy in Elementary Schools," *Teaching and Teacher Education* 12, no. 2 (1996): 179.

14. Ann Cook, "Parental Involvement," *Teacher Magazine* 5 (November–December 1993): 42−43.

15. J. L. Epstein, B. S. Simon, and K. C. Salinas, "Involving Parents in Homework in the Middle Grades," *Phi Delta Kappa Research Bulletin* 18 (September 1997): 1−4.

16. Ibid., 4.

17. Janet Chrispeels, *Homework and Home Learning Activities: Workshop Leader's Guide* (Washington, D.C.: U.S. Department of Education, Office of Educational Research and Improvement, 1996).

18. G. Natriello and E. McDill, "Performance Standards, Student Effort on Homework, and Academic Achievement," *Sociology of Education* 59 (1996): 18−31.

19. Gary Natriello, "Hoist on the Petard of Homework," *Teachers College Record* 98, no. 3 (spring 1997): 573.

20. McDermott, Goldman, and Varenne, "When School Goes Home," 398.

21. Ibid., 392.

22. Juliet B. Schor, *The Overworked American: The Unexpected Decline in Leisure* (New York: Basic Books, 1991). Author's estimates, from the 1988 Bureau of Labor Statistics, Office of Productivity and Technology, "Underlying Data for

Indexes of Output per Hour, Hourly Compensation, and Unit Labor Costs in Manufacturing, Twelve Industrial Countries, 1950–1988" (June 1989).

23. Clair Vickrey, "The Time-Poor: A New Look at Poverty," *The Journal of Human Resources* 12, no. 1 (winter 1977): 24–28.

24. Arlie Russell Hochschild, *The Second Shift* (New York: Avon, 1997).

25. Bureau of Labor Statistics, Current Population Survey, December 1999, available online. Figure on children in one-parent households is from the Children's Defense Fund web site.

26. Schor, *Overworked American*, 20–21.

27. Romesh Ratnesar, "The Homework Ate My Family," *Time,* January 25, 1999, 56.

28. Harris Cooper, *Homework* (White Plains, N.Y.: Longman, 1989).

29. D. A. England and J. K. Flatley, *Homework and Why* (Bloomington, Ind.: Phi Delta Kappa Educational Foundation, 1985).

30. Connecticut State Department of Education, *Attendance, Homework, Promotion, and Retention: A Manual of Policy Development and Administrative Procedures* (Hartford: Connecticut Department of Education, 1984), 22.

2. Does Homework Work?

1. Cooper, *Homework,* 12.

2. Ibid., 28.

3. Bill Barber, "Homework Does Not Belong on the Agenda for Educational Reform," *Educational Leadership* 43, no. 8 (May 1986): 56.

4. Ibid., 55.

5. Connecticut State Department of Education, *Manual on Policy Development,* 17.

6. Harris Cooper, "Synthesis of Research on Homework," *Educational Leadership* 47, no. 3 (1989): 89.

7. McDermott, Goldman, and Varenne, "When School Goes Home," 391–409.

8. W. C. Fredrick and H. J. Walberg, "Learning as a Function of Time," *Journal of Educational Research* 73 (March–April 1980), 183.

9. Harris M. Cooper, *The Battle over Homework: An Administrator's Guide to Setting Sound and Effective Policies* (Thousand Oaks, Calif.: Corwin Press, 1994), 27.

10. Ibid., 26–27.

11. Cooper, *Homework*, 91.

12. Charles Taylor, "Social Theory as Practice," in *Philosophical Papers*, vol. 2 (Cambridge: Cambridge University Press, 1985), 91–95.

13. We would like to see some broader survey research done on homework, and would suggest the inclusion of such questions as 1) How much time do your children or you spend each evening on homework? 2) How adequate do you feel in assisting your child with his/her homework? 3) What resources, space, etc., do you have available for that homework? 4) How much do you think your child learns from his/her homework 5) Are there other important skills or values your children are unlikely to acquire because of the time spent on homework? 6) Is having enough time for other activities, for you, your spouse, or your children, a major concern in your household?

We make no claim that any set of questions, including ours, is or could be ideologically neutral. But we do argue that respondents can and should have access to a set of broad arguments both for and against homework as precursors to such questions. Broad survey research in any form can never be a substitute for more in-depth interviewing, however limited the numbers we may reach through this latter method. Ethnographic studies are vital here, and some of these have been guided by the range of questions in which we have been interested. We have attempted to supplement these with some of our own. Ethnographic research methods are being used more frequently in the field of education as researchers strive to understand the ways in which the culture of schools is constructed. Called qualitative research, this methodology endeavors to uncover the meanings that individuals assign to their actions.

First developed by anthropologists as a way to study culture, ethnography focuses on the world of daily life and makes the familiar strange. By attending to the meanings given by participants to cultural ceremony and everyday life, ethnographers reveal and decode cultural phenomena. Ethnographic research demands close attention to detail, the recording of the minutiae of daily life, and in-depth interviews with various subjects. Ethnographers, often acting as participant observers, sometimes spend years in a setting studying one or two groups and the ways in which they create meaning out of their experience. This method is well suited for looking at students, especially those who are at risk of falling out of the system. Rather than presenting a statistic—e.g., "Thirty-four percent of the students in this district drop out"—ethnographers tell a story about one or two of those students whom they have followed around for some time. The result of this methodology is an ethnography that tells a story, albeit a partial one, about a particular subject—a story that has the potential both to elucidate and to elicit concerns common to the population under study as well as the one that reads the research.

Ethnographers have no claim to truth beyond the persuasiveness of the story they tell, on the ability both of the scholar and of the subject to inspire the shock of recognition when something in the story evokes in us dormant feelings or, at the very least, the sense that "there is more in heaven and earth than is dreamt of" in our traditional social science or policy narratives.

14. Gatto, *Dumbing Us Down*; Ann Cook, "Homework: Parent's Work, Kid's Work, or School Work?" *Education Week*, September 15, 1993, 30.

15. Helen Featherstone, "What Does Homework Accomplish?" *Principal* 65, no. 2 (November 1985): 6.

16. T. M. Rogers, "To Give or Not to Give: Homework," *NASSP Bulletin* 76 (October 1992): 13–15.

17. Martin Covington, "The Myth of Intensification," *Educational Researcher* 25, no. 8 (November 1996): 27–30.

18. National Education Summit, *National Education Summit Policy Statement* (1996).

19. Ibid.

20. Children's Defense Fund, *The State of America's Children: Yearbook 1997* (Washington, D.C.: Children's Defense Fund, 1997), 31.

21. Angela R. Taylor, "Conditions for American Children, Youth, and Families: Are We 'World Class'?" *Educational Researcher* 25, no. 8 (November 1996).

22. Ibid.

23. Taylor, "Conditions for American Children"; Gary Natriello, "Diverting Attention from Conditions in American Schools," *Educational Researcher* 25, no. 8 (November 1996), 7–9.

24. James Coleman et al., *Equality of Educational Opportunity* (Washington, D.C.: U.S. Department of Health, Education, and Welfare, 1966).

3. Homework in Historical Perspective

1. California Civil Code, 34th Session (1901), sec. 1665.

2. Brian Gill and Steve Schlossman, "A Sin against Childhood: Progressive Education and the Crusade to Abolish Homework, 1897–1941," *American Journal of Education* 105, no. 1 (November 1996): 30.

3. Ivan Illich, *Shadow Work* (Boston: Marion Boyars, 1981), 111–112.

4. Gill and Schlossman, "A Sin against Childhood."

5. Quoted in William H. Burnham, "The Hygiene of Home Study," *Pedagogical Seminary* 12 (June 1905): 213.

6. Vivian T. Thayer, *The Passing of Recitation* (Boston: D. C. Heath, 1928).

7. Edward Bok, "A National Crime at the Feet of American Parents," *Ladies' Home Journal* 17, no. 2 (January 1900): 16.

8. Ibid.

9. Edward Bok, "The First Blow," *LHJ* 17, no. 11 (October 1900): 16; idem, "First Step to Change the Public Schools," *LHJ* 31, no. 1 (January 1912): 3–4.

10. For examples of progressive thinking, see John Dewey, *The School and Society* (Chicago: University of Chicago Press, 1915); Carleton Washburne, "How Much Homework?" *Parent's Magazine* 12, no. 11 (November 1937): 16–17, 68–71.

11. William H. Holmes, "Home Work Is School Work Out of Place," *American Childhood* 152 (October 1929): 5–7, 55–56.

12. Clara Bassett, *The School and Mental Health* (New York: The Commonwealth Fund, 1934).

13. Dacie Harvey, "Too Much Homework," *New York Times*, April 4, 1935, 22.

14. Jay B. Nash, "At What Price Home Study?" *School Parent* 93, no. 5 (May 31, 1930): 6, 12.

15. Ethical Culture School, *Announcement of the Open Air Department of the Ethical Culture School*, New York, 1920–1921, 3.

16. Ibid., 6, 7.

17. Robert Rothschild, interview with Etta Kralovec, September 2, 1998.

18. John Dewey, *Democracy and Education: An Introduction to the Philosophy of Education* (New York: Macmillan, 1920).

19. The material on *Sputnik* is derived from Michael Sherry, *In the Shadow of War* (New Haven: Yale University Press, 1995), 214–233.

20. P. R. Wildman, "Homework Pressures," *Peabody Journal of Education* 45, no. 4 (January 1968): 204.

21. Ibid.

22. Romesh Ratnesar, "The Homework Ate My Family," *Time*, January 25, 1999.

23. Another recent article sensitively critiquing the perspective *A Nation at Risk* first elaborated regarding student and teacher inadequacies is "Blaming Teachers," *The American Prospect* 11, no. 2 (December 6, 1999): 40–45.

24. *A Nation at Risk: The Imperative of Educational Reform,* U.S. Department of Education, 1983, 5.

25. Ibid., 6.

4. Kids and Homework

1. *The Harare* [Zimbabwe] *Herald*, October 26, 1997. "In Hong Kong it is reported that elementary school students do three hours of homework a day. This has been correlated to suicides, such as 11-year-old Wong Ming-hung who jumped out of building, 34 stories to his death. His suicide note stated he was afraid to go back to school because his homework was undone." See also "Homework: To Your Books," *Economist*, May 6, 1995, 81.

2. Quoted in Pat Hinchey, "Why Kids Say They Don't Do Homework," *The Clearing House* 69, no. 4 (March–April 1996): 242.

3. Erik Erickson, *Identity, Youth and Crisis* (New York: Norton, 1968).

4. Ibid.

5. Hinchey, "Why Kids Say," 242.

6. Ibid., 243.

7. Ibid., 244.

8. Ibid.

9. Ibid., 245.

5. Homework and the Level Playing Field

1. E. C. Brooks, "The Value of Home Study under Parental Supervision," *Elementary School Journal* 17, no. 3 (November 1916): 193.

2. Cooper, *Homework*, 12.

3. Colin Greer, *The Great School Legend: A Revisionist Interpretation of American Public Education* (New York: Basic Books, 1972).

4. LouAnne Johnson, *My Posse Don't Do Homework* (New York: St. Martin's, 1992).

5. Jonathan Kozol, *Death at an Early Age: The Destruction of the Hearts and Minds of Negro Children in the Boston Public Schools* (Boston: Houghton Mifflin, 1967); Pat Conroy, *The Water Is Wide* (Boston: Houghton Mifflin, 1972); Susan Kammeraad-Campbell, *Teacher: Dennis Littky's Fight for a Better School* (New York: Plume, 1991); Deborah W. Meier, *The Power of Their Ideas: Lessons from a Small School in Harlem* (Boston: Beacon Press, 1995).

6. J. Coleman, E. Q. Campbell, C. J. Hobson, et al., *Equality of Educational Opportunity* (Washington, D.C.: U.S. Government Printing Office, 1966), 11.

7. Ibid.

8. See Coleman, et al., *Equality*, 12.

9. Jeannie Oakes, *Keeping Track: How Schools Structure Inequality* (New Haven: Yale University Press, 1985).

10. James Coleman, "The Concept of Equality of Educational Opportunity," *Harvard Educational Review* 38, no. 1 (winter 1968): 15.

11. Amy Stuart Wells and Irene Serna, "The Politics of Culture: Understanding Local Political Resistance to Detracking in Racially Mixed Schools," *Harvard Educational Review* 66, no. 1 (spring 1996): 93–118.

12. Coleman, "The Concept of Equality," 21–22.

13. Ibid.

14. Michael Apple, ed., *Cultural and Economic Reproduction in Education: Essays on Class, Ideology, and the State* (London: Routledge, 1982); Jay Macleod, *Ain't No Makin It: Leveled Aspirations in a Low-Income Neighborhood* (Boulder, Colo.: Westview Press, 1987).

15. Pierre Bourdieu, *Reproduction in Education, Society, and Culture* (London: Sage, 1990); Annette Lareau, *Home Advantage: Social Class and Parental Intervention in Elementary Education* (London: Falmer Press, 1989).

16. Samuel Bowles and Herbert Gintis, *Schooling in Capitalist America: Educational Reform and the Contradictions of Economic Life* (New York: Basic Books, 1976), 56.

17. Ibid., 132.

18. Ibid., 129.

19. Paul E. Willis, *Learning to Labor: How Working Class Kids Get Working Class Jobs* (Farnborough, England: Saxon House, 1977); Henry A. Giroux, *Theory and Resistance in Education: A Pedagogy for the Opposition* (London: Heinemann Educational Books, 1983).

20. Willis, *Learning to Labor.*

21. Oakes, *Keeping Track.*

22. Lareau, *Home Advantage.*

23. McDermott, Goldman, and Varenne, "When School Goes Home," 391–409.

6. Homework in the Global Economy

1. Schor, *Overworked American*, 152.

2. Lawrence Summers, quoted in *New York Times*, March 12, 1995, E5.

3. Kozol, *Savage Inequalities*.

4. Schor, *The Overspent American: Upscaling, Downshifting, and the New Consumer* (New York: Basic Books, 1998).

7. What's a Mother—and a Neighborhood, and a Nation—to Do?

1. Children's Defense Fund, *The State of America's Children 1997*.

2. Anne Cassidy, *Parents Who Think Too Much: Why We Do It, How to Stop* (New York: Dell, 1998), front cover.

3. Harve Varenne and R. McDermott, *Successful Failure: The School America Builds* (Boulder, Colo.: Westview Press, 1998).

4. C. Wright Mills, "The Big City: Private Troubles and Public," in *Power, Politics and People: The Collected Essays of C. Wright Mills*, ed. Irving Louis Horowitz (London: Oxford University Press, 1963), 395–402.

5. C. Wright Mills, "Women: The Darling Little Slaves," in *Power, Politics, and People*, 339–342.

6. D. Meier, *The Power of Their Ideas*.

ACKNOWLEDGMENTS

Our book about homework began almost a decade ago, where any solid work on this subject must, with students. At the time, we were conducting a research project for the state of Maine on dropout prevention programs. We never imagined that we would end up with a book on homework. As part of that study, a graduate student at College of the Atlantic, Bridget Mullen, conducted over forty in-depth interviews with high school dropouts.

We all had a hunch that there was a moment when kids knew they weren't going to make it through school, and we were interested in finding out what that moment was. In response to the question "When did you know you weren't going to make it through school," all the students told a story that included their inability to complete homework assignments! These students and others who shared their frustrations about homework and hopes for the future gave birth to this book.

As we were grappling with our findings about homework, our own family lives seemed to converge on the topic. Both of us had young children who were imaginative, curious, and conscientious. Nevertheless, we found that homework both exhausted them and limited their opportunities to pursue their own projects. In most cases, we as parents couldn't help thinking that those childhood interests and passions were at least as compelling as anything the school was demanding. We talked to other parents and began to see that many had the same struggles and frustrations over the intrusion of homework into their family lives.

Conversations with COA colleagues John Visvader, John Anderson, Davis Taylor, Suzanne Morse, Rich Borden, and Alesia

Maltz both challenged our assumptions and helped us further develop our insights. We became convinced that we had the makings of a book that placed homework in the context of the evolution of class bias in the public schools, the modern corporate workplace, and long-standing cultural attitudes toward work and the young. Supportive comments from Stanley Aronowitz encouraged us to pursue further the connections between long workplace hours and the intensification of homework.

Throughout the preparation of the manuscript, we were once again able to draw on student assistance. Bridget's contribution to the research design and her sensitivity to the students elicited many thoughtful and provocative responses. We doubt this project would ever have seen the light of day without her hard work. Melinda Magleby, a student at College of the Atlantic, served as our research assistant for the last year of our manuscript preparation. She brought to the task a thorough grasp of our themes and an equal willingness to probe our logic and our agenda. We are very much in her debt. Students in our classes at College of the Atlantic offered challenges and stories of their own that enriched our understandings.

Finally, Beacon Press has played a major role in our work, and we would like to thank Beacon director Helene Atwan.

Our hope for this project is that it will add to a growing national conversation. The comments and criticisms of concerned readers in all walks of life have aided us at every stage of this project, and we are confident that publication of this work will enhance the dialogue.

Etta Kralovec and John Buell

I would like to thank the teachers and administrators of Union #98 on Mount Desert Island, Maine, especially Judith Cox, who challenged me and engaged in ongoing conversations over the years this book was in process. Their insights and questions brought the subject to life. I also often turned to Beverly Paigen and Steve Mooser for invaluable technical advice. Early on, Donna Gold had an interest in the topic, and through her hard questions helped me shape many of my ideas. The Wheeler family shared their stories with me and convinced me the I was on to something deeply important for families. The insights and questions of my family and friends pushed to me think more deeply about this topic. I would especially like to acknowledge my husband, Frank Davis, who has persuaded me to see the world from a different point of view and has helped me understand this topic in new ways.

EK

Over two decades ago, Sam Bowles and the other editors of *Dollars and Sense* first convinced me that school reform and corporate reform are inseparable projects. I owe them a continuing intellectual debt. I also acknowledge the support and encouragement of my father-in-law, Tony Covino, a former K-8 principal, and my mother-in-law, Mary Covino, a former elementary school teacher. Both have long harbored doubts about homework and encouraged me to express mine. I also especially acknowledge the contribution of my wife, Susan Covino Buell, who first made me aware of this issue. In her tenure on the local school board she set a courageous example by expressing concerns about the role homework plays in perpetuating inequality.

JB

socioeconomic class: and diversified curriculum, 73; and economic mobility,
70–71; and factors associated with,
68; general differences in, 70; and
impact of global economy on, 82–
86; as indicator of academic success,
37, 65–66; lower, and disadvanta-
geous effects of homework, 70–71,
101; and public schools, 69–71; and
residential segregation in schools,
74–75; and role of schools in repro-
ducing class structure, 77–78, 101;
and tracking, 78–80
Sputnik, 46–47, 48
SRC. *See* University of Michigan's Survey Research Center
Stillman, Bessie, 45
stress: of balancing homework and
other activities, 1; of doing homework, 2, 61
suicide and role of school pressure in, 49
Summers, Lawrence, 82
support services, 67
survey research, suggested questions for:
91, 106–7n13

taxes, property, and impact on residential segregation of schools, 75, 84
teachers: and challenges in impover-
ished communities, 72; as expert
trainers of children, 44; and feelings
about homework, 14–15, 34; as
members of middle class, 77; and
need for alliances with parents, 95;
and reasons given for assigning
homework, 35–36
Teachers Involve Parents in Schoolwork
(TIPS), 15–16
technology, call for broader use of, 36
television, 100

Terkel, Studs, 48
time, 19–21; and international comparisons of study, 9; and leisure as a commodity, 19, 86; management of, 2,
13, 14; as reason for not doing homework, 56
time poverty, 19
TIPS. *See* Teachers Involve Parents in
Schoolwork
Title One programs, 76
Title Two programs, 76
tracking, 66, 78; and college competition, 79; and homework, 79–80; as
means of reinforcing socioeconomic
class structure, 78–79

United States: and competition with
Russia, 46–48; and governmental
support of educational programs, 16
United States Department of Educa-
tion, 16
University of Michigan's Survey
Research Center (SRC), 20

Walker, Francis A., 42
women, increased demand upon, 6, 19
"work and spend": as a cycle in families,
19–20, 86, 100; as an American
means to gain identity, 86; and how
to curb current pressures on workers,
89
work ethic, American, 69; homework's
support of, 7; and self-discipline, 12,
35; and teachers' support of, 69
work hours, 19
workplace, conventional corporate, 85–
86
"workplace, high-performance," 84–85;
and lack of implementation in
United States, 85